CPI Antony Rowe
Eastbourne, UK
November 08, 2019

BREW

British
Real Ale

Graham Wheeler

BOOKS

Published by the Campaign for Real Ale Ltd
230 Hatfield Road
St Albans
Hertfordshire AL1 4LW
www.camra.org.uk/books
© Campaign for Real Ale 2009
3rd edition published 2009
Reprinted with minor corrections 2009
Reprinted 2010, 2011, 2012

ISBN 978-1-85249-258-8

A CIP catalogue record for this book is available
from the British Library
Printed and bound in Slovenia by Latitude Press Ltd

Managing Editor: Simon Hall
Project Editor: Katie Hunt
Editorial Assistance: Emma Haines
Design/Typography: Stephen Bere
Copy Editor: Ione Brown
Indexer: Hilary Bird
Head of Marketing: Tony Jerome

Cover photography
Above far left: **Shutterstock/Valentyn Volkov,** Above left: **Shut-
terstock/argonaut,** Above right: **Shutterstock/Supertrooper,**
Above far right: **www.brouland.com,** Main picture: **Alamy/Food-
folio.** Back cover: **CAMRA archive**

Contents

Introduction

IT HAS BEEN SOME YEARS SINCE I wrote the previous edition of *Brew Your Own...* Much has changed since then and this updated version attempts to address some of the recent developments in the hobby.

Not only do we now have better-quality ingredients, but a full range of commercially-made equipment is available to us, saving us from having to make it ourselves. Techniques have become more standardised and the quality of home-brewed beer has improved enormously. Compromises were inevitable in home-brewing, even eight years ago when the last edition was published. There is no need to compromise these days.

The commercial world has changed as well. Many breweries have closed and their beers are contract-brewed elsewhere. Other breweries have been taken over and brewing transferred to the parent company. New micro-breweries have sprung up, while many others have gone to the wall. There is no doubt that British commercial brewing will never be the same again after recent takeovers and mergers made in the name of money.

This revised guide focuses on providing commercial-standard recipes for traditional beers, reflecting current best British home-brewing practice and presenting it to the reader in a simple manner.

These home-brewing methods are based on traditional commercial brewing practice because that most closely reflects the way home-brewers brew today. An essay on home-brewing published by William Cobbett in 1821 shows that little has changed in 200 years. Indeed, Cobbett's instructions are better and more practical in many respects than many of the home-brewing texts published after the modern revival of home-brewing in the 1960s.

Up until the last quarter of the 20th century, commercial brewing was in fact little different from home-brewing. Many of the *traditional* regional breweries brewed in the same way that they had for generations, using the same vessels that were installed when their brewery was built, often 200 years earlier. Stainless steel, computer-controlled, fully automated brew houses, built for economy of production rather than quality of product, are almost a 21st-century evil, although the big mega-keggeries started the trend in the 1960s.

Despite the closure of so many of the small, highly-respected regional breweries over the last 20 years or so, there are still a few survivors that brew in the traditional way using their age-old equipment. The traditional brewers such as Hook Norton and Palmers of Bridport, among others, brew in exactly the same way that home-brewers do – proper mash tuns, open fermentation and the like. The main difference is that they use bigger buckets than we do.

It must be stated that the recipes here attempt to *emulate* well-known British beers – not to duplicate them. The recipes will rarely be identical to the commercial equivalents, even though they are based on information that the brewers themselves freely divulged. It would be an almost impossible task to duplicate the beers because no recipe is ever fixed, but changes from year to year and evolves, particularly at the time of writing when last year's crops were hit hard by bad weather, creating shortages of both barley and hops. Many brewers have been forced to modify their recipes to take advantage of the varieties of malted barley and, in particular, hops that are available at a reasonable price. But equating a recipe with a well-known beer is a good way of choosing a beer of the style that you enjoy, and the recipes should succeed in that.

Many of the original recipes remain from the previous edition, although updated. Some new recipes have been added, some removed, and the remainder adjusted to reflect the currently-published specification of the commercial equivalent.

This is basically a recipe book, so there is not a lot of technical brewing information within the text. I have kept it relatively simple to avoid frightening people off by making the task appear more complicated than it really is.

Brewing at home is much easier than it sounds when reading about it in a book. The malt extract method is particularly easy; almost child's play. The full mash method is a little more complicated, requires more equipment and takes a lot longer, but the rewards are greater. Whichever method you choose, I wish you success and happy brewing!

Graham Wheeler

Home-brewing Methods

Brewing is fundamentally a natural process. The brewer's art is in converting natural products into a pleasing beverage – namely malted barley and hops into ale. A brief outline of the process is as follows:

Stage 1

The brewing process begins with *mashing*, which involves mixing crushed malted barley (*grist*) and hot water (*liquor*) to make a sloppy porridge (the *mash*). This porridge is held at a fairly constant temperature of around 66°C for about 90 minutes. This extracts sugars from the malted barley. After the 90-minute standing period the liquid is drained from the mash and a process known as *sparging* begins. Sparging is brewer-speak for rinsing, and this entails slowly sprinkling hot liquor over the grains to rinse out entrapped sugars.

Stage 2

The sugary liquid is then transferred to a boiler, which brewers usually call a *copper*. It is boiled for 90 minutes along with a quantity of hops. The boil sterilises the liquid, now called *wort*, and causes unwanted excessive protein to coagulate and settle out. The hops provide additional flavour and aroma, and add preservative properties to the beer.

When the boiling period is over, the wort is cooled and transferred to a fermenting vessel. Yeast is added and fermentation begins. Fermentation converts the majority of the sugar into alcohol and takes about five days.

The beer is then transferred to cask and matured for a period for the flavours to mellow and round out. It is then ready for consumption.

With home-brewing we have the choice of performing the full process, which includes stage 1 and stage 2 (full mash brewing) or we can use a simplified method where stage 1 is performed for us in a factory, and we just perform stage 2 (malt extract brewing).

As home-brewers we can either buy the malt as grain and brew our own fully-mashed, all-grain beers, or we can use malt extract. Mashing from grain produces the best quality beers and gives the brewer total control over his process, whereas malt extract eliminates the need for mashing and is more convenient. All of the recipes in this book are designed for mashing, and many of them have a malt extract version too. You can brew using your own preferred method.

Malt extract brewing – no mash required

Malt extract is certainly the most convenient way of brewing – it knocks an hour or two off the brewing process when compared to brewing from grain (full mash), and you do not need as much equipment. It is very easy to do – no more difficult than making up a beer kit. You do not usually even need to bother about water treatment. Malt extract will produce convenient, palatable beers, but many people believe that an extract beer does not compare with a fully-mashed beer in terms of quality and flavour.

While a well-made mashed beer will always have the edge over an extract beer, not everyone has the time or equipment required to mash. Few people realise that top quality beers can be produced at home using malt extract.

All of the ingredients are simply boiled vigorously for an hour or so and then strained into the fermentation bin. However, with this simple boil-up method the brewer is restricted in the range of ingredients that he can use. Only those ingredients that do not require enzymic conversion (which occurs during mashing) can be used. Apart from malt extract; crystal malt, chocolate malt, black malt, roast barley, and a fair range of speciality malts can be used. Cereal adjuncts should not be used, but this is not a serious disadvantage. Many beer buffs regard the use of adjuncts as adulteration anyway, and the use of adjuncts in commercial beer is becoming rare. The complete range of brewing sugars and syrups can be used.

Many of the recipes in this book can be brewed using this method. Full instructions are given on *p71*.

Fully mashed beers

With a fully mashed beer the fermentable sugars are produced from crushed malted barley grain. Mashing from grain requires more equipment than extract brewing – a mash tun, or at least a grain bag, will be required. It also requires more care and attention, and it will take about a day to make a brew. Nevertheless, it is well worth the effort. Brewing from grain is the best way to emulate the commercial recipes in this book because that is what the breweries themselves do. Mashing produces distinctive, quality beers, and is the only technique that gives the brewer complete and flexible control over his product.

It may seem to take a leap of faith to enter into fully-mashed or all-grain brewing, but it is far easier in practice than it appears on paper. Admittedly it is a good idea to get some brewing experience first by brewing with a beer kit or malt extract to get the fundamentals of brewing under your belt.

Read the step-by-step, full-mash brewing instructions in this book, and you are ready to go. Start off with a basic recipe and do not mess around with much in the way of water treatment initially – that will come later. Half the battle with full-mash brewing is psychological – there's nothing like actually doing it to get your head round the process.

All of the recipes in this book can be brewed using the full mash method. Instructions are provided on *p73*.

Fermentable Ingredients

The primary ingredient of beer is barley; malted barley to be precise. Malted barley, or malt, is barley that has been soaked in water and allowed to germinate. When the germination has proceeded far enough, it is halted by drying the malt. The malt is then kilned to ensure that it is dried properly and brought to the desired colour.

Malts for brewing

Listed below are the malts and other ingredients used in the recipes.

The darker ingredients impart a darker colour to the beer, but the subject of colour is very woolly and not worth losing much sleep over. The reason for specifying colour is so that you know which product to go for when confronted with a choice – there is a much wider range of ingredients available than those specified here. The colours are given in EBC (European Brewing Convention) units. Colour specifications for darker malts vary considerably betwen maltsters, and there are large tolerance spreads on top of that, due to the difficulty of kilning to precise colours. Where there is a wide tolerance spread, the figure in brackets is the one used in recipe calculations.

Pale malt

The primary ingredient in most English beers, this is simply malted barley, lightly kilned during drying to provide a very light colour. Pale malt can be purchased whole or crushed; it must be crushed before use in the mash tun.
Colour: **5 EBC**

Extra pale malt

This is pale malt that has been very lightly kilned to produce a lighter-coloured malt. It is a popular ingredient in the new generation of very light 'summer' ales.
Colour: **2.5 EBC**

Mild ale malt

Mild ale malt is made from higher-nitrogen barley than pale malt. This allows it to be kilned to a darker colour than pale malt without reducing its diastatic activity (enzymatic power). A higher level of diastatic activity is required in order to assist in the conversion of the high levels of adjuncts that are typical of Mild ales. Mild ale malt can be purchased whole or crushed; it must be crushed before use in the mash tun.

Colour: **7 EBC**

Amber malt

Amber malt is made by kilning mild ale malt at 100-150°C until the desired amber colour is reached. It is then removed from the kiln and allowed to cool. It gives beer a dry biscuity flavour and a rich golden colour. Amber malt can be purchased whole or crushed; it must be crushed before use in the mash tun. The colour of this stuff varies considerably from maltster to maltster.

Colour: **40-80 EBC (60)**

Chocolate malt

Chocolate malt is a malt that has been kilned to a very dark colour. It is used to give flavour and colour to dark beers: Milds, Stouts and Porters. Popular in winter ales, it gives rich, dark colour with burnt toast dryness. Chocolate malt can be purchased whole or crushed; it should be crushed before use in the mash tun. It can be used in the copper for malt extract beers.

Colour: **900-1200 EBC (1050)**

Black malt

Black malt, as the name implies, is malted barley that has been kilned to a high degree, turning the malt black. It is used for flavour and colour. Black malt does not need to mashed. It is used in the mash tun for convenience, but it can be used in the copper when brewing from malt extract.

Colour: **1200-1400 EBC (1300)**

Roasted barley

Roasted barley is unmalted barley that has been roasted until it is black. It is used to impart a unique dry, burnt flavour to dry Stouts. Its use promotes a thick Guinness-style head. Roasted barley does not need to mashed; it is used in the mash tun for convenience, but it can be used in the copper when brewing from malt extract.

Colour: **1000-1400 EBC (1350)**

Crystal malt

Crystal malt is made by wetting high-nitrogen malt and holding it at 65°C in an enclosed vessel. The grains are then dried at temperatures of around 250°C. Crystal malt does not need to be mashed; it is used in the mash tun for convenience, but it can be used in the copper when brewing from malt extract. These days, crystal malt is available in various colours: typically standard, light and dark. Light-coloured crystal malt imparts a sweetness, whereas darker varieties progressively impart more complex flavours ranging from toffee through to malty to burnt. The recipes usually use standard crystal malt.

Standard: **130-170 EBC (150)**
Light: **50-70 EBC (60)**
Dark: **200-400 EBC (300)**

Wheat malt

Wheat malt is an increasingly popular ingredient in British beers. It gives a unique flavour and even a small addition can enhance head formation and retention.

Colour: **3-4 EBC (3.5)**

Cereal adjuncts

Torrefied wheat, flaked wheat, flaked maize and flaked barley are the adjuncts most commonly used in British beers, particularly Milds. They all impart subtly different flavours and characteristics to the beers. They do not impart colour and do not need to be crushed.

Malt extract syrup

Malt extract syrup, sometimes referred to as liquid malt extract, is a gooey substance that comes in a can. It is made from malted barley and is used as a substitute for it. The mashing stage is performed at the factory, saving the brewer from having to do it himself, thereby speeding up the brewing process. Malt extract does need to be boiled for the full period of 60 or 90 minutes as appropriate, just as is the case for fully-mashed beers.

The recipes here that include a malt extract version require extra pale (or extra light) malt extract syrup of around 5.5 EBC in colour. The colour of the finished beer, if darker, is provided by additional ingredients in the recipe.

A good tip if you are uncomfortable weighing sticky fluids is to use a graduated jug. One kilogram of malt extract syrup occupies 0.71 litres (710 ml) – so, simply multiply the weight by 0.71. A recipe that calls for 3,500 grams of malt extract would require 2,485 ml of the stuff. Ensure that the scale on your jug is accurate – usually they are not.

Dried malt extract

Dried malt extract, or malt extract powder, starts off life as a syrup, but is then subjected to a process that removes most of the water to form a sticky, hydroscopic powder.

There has been much discussion as to whether or not dried malt extract produces the same quality of beer as malt extract syrup – the argument being that the additional processing must remove something other than water. It is probably true that top-quality malt extract syrup will produce superior beer. However, certain reactions slowly take place in the container during storage and this reaction causes what is known as the 'malt extract tang'. Therefore, only fresh malt extract syrup will produce superior beer. With the dried extract this reaction is halted by the drying process and therefore it has much better keeping qualities and the malt extract tang is not an issue.

What is true is that dried malt extract will produce a better beer than malt extract syrup that is not absolutely fresh. The powder is easier to handle and weigh, easier to store (no half-used tins of syrup to store or go off), and has a couple of years' shelf life. Dried malt extract has a number of other uses around the brewery: making yeast starters (see p32), making priming solutions (see p80), making emergency adjustments to gravity and so on, so it is always useful to have some in stock.

When mixing dried malt extract into the liquor (water) in the boiler, do it at a low enough temperature to ensure that there is no steam issuing from the surface to be absorbed by the extract, causing it to form lumps. Add it gradually while stirring. The recipes in this book require extra-pale or extra-light dried malt extract of about 5.5 EBC. The powder should be stored sealed, in a warm, dry place.

Brewing sugars

All brewing sugars and syrups are known as copper sugars or copper syrups because they are added to the copper during the boil. They do not need mashing and are not added to the mash tun. They can be used with equal success in grain brewing or malt extract brewing.

Commercial brewers have a bewildering array of brewing sugars available to them. The sugars are derived from a number of sources, have varying degrees of fermentability and come in various colours. There are a number of home-brew products available in powder, liquid and sticky-chip form that are spuriously labelled 'brewing sugar', 'glucose' or some other vague term. Very often, however, it is not clear from the label what the product actually is: it could be any one of a dozen different forms of sugar.

In this book, the recipes have been reformulated to do away with specialist brewing sugars because of the difficulty in obtaining them through home-brewing sources. Also, these days, few commercial brewers use specialist sugars, apart from invert

sugar, and that can be substituted with household sugar.

Invert cane sugar

Brewers rarely use ordinary cane sugar, but instead use invert cane sugar. Cane sugar (sucrose) consists of equal parts of glucose and fructose which are bonded together molecularly. Yeast can secrete an enzyme (invertase) which breaks these molecular bonds and splits the sugar into its two component types. However, yeast needs to break these bonds before it can ferment the sugars. Invert cane sugar is sucrose that has had the molecular bonds already broken by an industrial process, which saves the yeast from doing it. Ordinary cane sugar can be used in place of invert with no difference to the home-brewer, except perhaps in colour. Brewers have traditionally used invert sugar because they feel that ordinary sugar gives a 'sugar tang' to the finished beer, and causes disproportionate hangovers. Whether or not this is true is a matter of conjecture, but I can believe it.

Invert cane sugar can be in the form of sticky blocks, chunks or syrup. It is available to commercial brewers in four colours from No. 1 to No. 4 – 1 being the lightest and 4 black. Invert sugar, like ordinary sugar, is 100 per cent fermentable and leaves no residual sweetness or body in a beer. Tate & Lyle Golden Syrup is partially inverted cane sugar. The recipes in this book specify ordinary domestic cane white sugar in place of invert sugar. It can be freely substituted.

Hops

The variety and quantity of hops, and the stage at which they are added to a beer, greatly influence the end result and determine the major distinguishing characteristics between similar styles of beer from different breweries. They provide any beer with the greater part of its individuality. These days there are a great many varieties of hop which can be used in any combination and quantity, at various stages of the brewing process, to impart this individuality.

The hop characteristic of a beer is the most difficult quality to emulate and provides the most variable aspect of beer production. Hops are ingredients of the most inconsistent quality and they are heavily influenced by weather conditions and agronomy. The characteristics of the same hop variety, grown in the same region, differ from year to year due to annual variations in climate. They are also affected by day length – the same variety of hop grown in another region will display subtly different characteristics and will exhibit different yields.

Hop flavour and bitterness diminish with age in storage. Hop utilisation efficiency – how well the hops are utilised during the brewing process – is partly determined by the process. The vigour of the boil, the length of the boil, the original gravity of the beer, even boiler geometry affect utilisation. It follows that to emulate the hop character of a specific beer is no easy matter.

To complicate matters further, at the time of writing (2008) there is a serious world-wide hop shortage due to poor weather conditions that struck most of the major hop-growing regions of the world before the 2007 harvest. Many popular hops are either unavailable or prohibitively expensive. Strange hops with even stranger names are being imported from all sorts of unlikely places in an attempt to offset the shortage. This has forced brewers to change their hop varieties to whatever is available on the market at the right price and hope that the resultant changes to their beers are not sufficient to put their regular customers off.

Hopefully, normality will be restored by the time this book is published and brewers will have reverted to their preferred varieties. Some will not, of course, because they will be afraid of suddenly changing the characteristics of their beer yet again; others may find that their beer is more popular with the substitutes and will decide to stick with them. The recipes in the book quote the brewers' preferred varieties even though some may not be using them at the moment.

Commercial brewers often substitute and blend hops on an almost continuous basis to take advantage of varying market prices and seasonal differences in hop quality. A brewer's hop recipe is rarely rigidly fixed and diversions from the standard recipes are common and happen anyway even without a hop shortage.

Hop components

There are three main components supplied by hops: alpha acid, beta acid and essential oils. The two that we are mostly interested in are alpha acid and essential oils. Alpha acid supplies bitterness and preservative properties. Essential oils supply flavour and aroma. As is often the case in brewing, there is a snag: alpha acid is difficult to get into solution and requires a long boil to do so – anything up to two hours. Essential oils, however, are volatile and quickly driven off with the steam when boiling – a long boil will drive off the majority of the aroma. The two requirements are not compatible. This leads to the practice of brewers adding hops at two or more stages during the brewing process. Bittering hops are added at the beginning of the boil and aroma hops added at the end.

Alpha acid

Alpha acid is the primary bittering component of the hop. It is in fact one of the insoluble resins present in hops. Being insoluble, alpha acid is difficult to get into solution, but with a prolonged boil the alpha acid becomes isomerised – converted into iso-alpha acid, which is far more soluble. Isomerisation is a slow process and requires a long boil to complete. It is usual to boil the wort for at least 90 minutes for isomerisation to complete and for the alpha acid to be solubilised.

Different varieties of hop contain different amounts of alpha acid and thus different bittering powers. Also, the alpha acid content of any specific hop variety varies from season to season, from harvest to harvest, and from growing region to growing region. Furthermore, the alpha acid content will diminish during storage due to oxidation. This means that determining bitterness and maintaining consistent bitterness in a commercial beer is quite an art form. Hop merchants provide the maximum and minimum alpha acid content that can be expected for each variety in their published data, and the mean of these can be used mathematically to approximate bitterness in the absence of better information.

The alpha acid content of each harvest is measured by hop merchants to evaluate quality, and this information is supplied to commercial brewers as the basis for purchasing the hops. Sometimes this information filters down to the home-brew hobby and a specific figure for alpha acid content (often abbreviated as AA) is printed on some home-brew packets of hops. Analytical techniques used to measure alpha acid are not particularly precise: different methods give differing results for the same hop. Humanly-perceived bitterness is quite different from machine-measured bitterness which is again quite different from calculated bitterness, and in the end it comes down to taste. Then there is hop utilisation, another minefield of a subject which provides yet more variation and unknowns.

It is becoming common in home-brewing communities to treat alpha acid and beer bitterness as a precise science. All sorts of complicated formulae, tables and other mathematical tools exist that claim to calculate the bitterness of a beer from the alpha acid figures for the hops used. However, the accuracy of that data is questionable and it is unreasonable to expect any degree of precision from these mathematical predictions.

It should always be borne in mind that the primary reason for hop merchants specifying alpha acid levels is to give a comparative yardstick as to their market price. A commercial brewer will not be prepared to pay the same price per tonne for a batch of hops containing 4% alpha acid as he would for the same variety containing 5% alpha acid using the same analytical method. The ability to approximate bitterness from this figure is a bonus to home-brewers,

but calculating bitterness is not the hop merchant's motive for doing it. Bitterness calculation from alpha acid content is a useful approximation it must be said, but it remains an approximation just the same.

Beta acid

It is generally suggested among home-brewing types that beta acid does not contribute to the bitterness of a beer. This is, in fact, untrue. In its fresh state beta acid does not contribute to bitterness, but oxidised beta acid does. It is an ageing thing. As hops get older the resins oxidise, which has the effect of reducing the bittering power of alpha acid but increasing the bittering power of beta acid.

Beta acid is usually ignored in any hop calculations as in fresh hops the beta acid does not contribute to bitterness and in older hops the beta acid tends to compensate for loss of alpha acid.

Essential oils

Essential oils are a group of alcohol-like compounds with around 200 components that provide hop flavour and aroma. These components react with one another to produce the range of flavours and aromas that can be detected in a beer. Essential oils are volatile and the majority of these are driven off during a prolonged boil, thus those beers that are expected to have a hoppy flavour or aroma often need a quantity of best-quality aroma hops added late in the boil, post boil, or in the cask to provide this quality.

The volatility of essential oils is variable – different components boil away at different times and temperatures. This means that some components have more 'stickability' in the wort than others. The aroma components – by definition highly volatile if you can smell them – are more readily driven off than the flavour components. Therefore the flavour and aroma differences between hops added at different stages can be readily detected.

Late hops – those that are given a short boil – mostly contribute flavour, with some of the aroma fractions boiled off depending on the length of boil. Post-boil hops, added to the hot wort after the boil has stopped, contribute mostly aroma and lower levels of flavour. Dry hops, added to the cask, contribute aroma and little or no flavour. These variations provide yet more opportunity to express individuality in any beer.

Hop types

Many brewers, commercial brewers in particular, reckon that alpha acid is just alpha acid and that it supplies bittering but not flavour; the flavour and aroma components get driven off by the length of the boil. This is not strictly true – a subject to be discussed later – nevertheless, this has lead to the development of high-alpha hops intended purely for bittering. These are hops designed to have exceptionally high levels of alpha acid and high yields in the hop

garden. This makes them more economical to buy and use in the brewhouse, therefore more attractive to brewery accountants.

The snag is that high-alpha hops often have an objectionable flavour and aroma and are not suitable for flavour and aroma additions. This has lead to different classes of hops being grown: bittering hops and aroma hops. A third type exists known as dual-purpose hops. These are high- or moderately-high-alpha acid hops with good bittering powers that are deemed (by the hop merchants at least) to have a sufficiently delicate aroma to also be useful as aroma hops.

The traditional old-fashioned varieties – Goldings, Fuggles and their derivatives – are still regarded as the best hops, even for bittering, and the best beers use them exclusively. After 100 years of hop development, nobody has bettered them. However, if all the brewers who claim to use just traditional varieties really did so, our hop gardens would be full of Fuggles and Goldings, but they are not.

Bittering hops (primary hops, copper hops)

Bittering hops are those that are put into the copper at the beginning of the boil for bittering and preservation purposes. Alpha acid is the primary bittering component of a hop, and it follows that high-alpha hops are the most economical bittering hops, although any variety of hop can be used for bittering. Indeed, high-alpha hops often give a degree of harshness. The highest quality beers use low-alpha, traditional hops for bittering, such as Fuggles and Golding, which are much more mellow.

High-alpha hops are usually hybrids, bred specially for high alpha acid content, high yields and dense cropping in the hop garden. The high yields make them cheaper to buy and their high alpha acid content makes them economical to use in the copper. A hop such as Target has nearly three times the alpha acid of, say, a Fuggle, therefore only a third of the quantity of Target will be required to achieve the same degree of bitterness imparted by Fuggles.

There are dangers, however, in using high-alpha hops for bittering, due to the harshness and poor flavours that these can impart. The essential oils get distilled off in the boil, but some of the flavour remains through to the bitter end, so to speak. This is, perhaps, not so significant in lightly-hopped beers where the harshness may not be detectable, nor might it be significant in beers where the harshness is masked by other flavours, such as roast malts. However, in heavily hopped beers such as Bitters or IPAs, the harshness does become objectionable and, to overcome this, high-alpha hops are often blended with other varieties or avoided altogether. There is, apparently, no scientific or biological reason why a high-alpha hop cannot have a pleasant flavour or aroma, it's just that nobody has achieved it yet.

Aroma hops

Aroma hops are those varieties of hop that are considered to have a fine flavour and aroma. Indeed, aroma hops are mostly the traditional, old-fashioned hop varieties such as Fuggles and Goldings, or their derivatives, that were used by traditional British breweries up until the 1960s. Traditional varieties are still preferred as aroma hops because they display the true, authentic, English hop character.

These hops can also be used as bittering hops, and the finest quality beers do employ aroma hops for bittering, as did almost all British beers until modern high-alpha hops emerged. Goldings and Fuggles are considered to be the finest aroma hops but they have low yields, low alpha acid and low disease resistance, and are therefore more expensive to a commercial brewer than modern, intensively-farmed, high yield, disease-resistant hybrids.

Aroma hops are usually employed as late hops, added to the copper in the last few minutes of the boil; as post-boil hops, added to the hot wort when boiling has ceased; or as dry hops, added to the cask after filling. Many breweries use the new dual-purpose hops for all or part of their aroma. Hop growers claim that all the hybrid varieties of hop, with the possible exception of Target, have a pleasing aroma, but that is a matter of opinion.

Dual-purpose hops

These are new hybrid varieties that have been developed especially for high yields and disease resistance, but with a moderate to high alpha acid content and a sufficiently delicate aroma to be used as a copper hop or aroma hop. Challenger is the most common dual-purpose hop used in this country, followed closely by Northdown. Northdown is a replacement for the old Northern Brewer variety.

Hop flavour and aroma

The subject of hop flavour and aroma is itself worthy of discussion. Not all hops have a pleasant flavour or aroma; indeed the flavour of some hops can be regarded as obnoxious. Although aroma hops can be used at the start of the boil for bittering purposes, and the very best beers do exclusively use aroma hops for bittering, the converse is not true. High-alpha bittering hops should not be used late to impart aroma. In my view, few, if any, high-alpha hops are suitable for late hopping, but many large brewers do use them for that purpose. It is a regrettable fact that some hop flavours and aromas regarded as acceptable today would not have been given house room 20 or 30 years ago.

The reason that poorly-flavoured hops are becoming acceptable is that they are being forced upon the public and people are getting used

to them. High-alpha, high-yield hops are cheaper to buy, and the majority of British hop gardens are devoted to high-alpha hops. Hop acreage in Britain is declining rapidly. The tendency for British hop farmers to grub up their hop gardens and plant more profitable, easier to grow, cash crops, means that large quantities of hops are now imported. Alpha acid can be traded on the world market as a commodity; flavour is not so easy because of national preferences. Major breweries today buy alpha, not flavour.

Many breweries, particularly micro-breweries, are now experimenting with imported hops, usually American, that impart a high level of spiciness that is not a traditional characteristic of British beers. They use them to give their beers a degree of distinction, particularly in seasonal specials.

Hop additions

As mentioned earlier, it is quite common for commercial and home-brewers to add hops at different stages of the brewing process to impart various characteristics. All beers have primary hops – those that are added at the beginning of the boil to impart bitterness – but by no means all beers have hops added at a later stage. Only those beers that are expected to have a predominant hop flavour need to be late hopped, and then only those that are relatively lightly hopped anyway.

Late hopping and post-boil hopping are appropriate for pale ales and Bitters, but the benefits are most apparent in relatively lightly-hopped beers; in heavily hopped or very bitter beers enough flavour is likely to be carried across from the primary hops and, besides, the bitterness may mask the delicate hop flavour that the technique imparts. Hop aroma can be added by dry hopping, which is much more common. There is no need to adopt late hopping or even dry hopping for Milds, Stouts, or any beer in which a predominant hop flavour is not an outstanding feature or would be masked by other assertive flavours.

Primary hops

These are the hops put into the copper to give bitterness. Such hops require around 90 minutes vigorous boiling for the alpha acids to become isomerised and dissolve into the wort, thus imparting bitterness. The mechanical action of a vigorous boil helps rupture the lupulin glands of the hop and so assist in isomerisation. Any type of hop can be used at this stage. It is up to the preferred practice of the brewer as to when he adds these to the copper, and it matters little, as long as the hops receive their full boiling period.

Some home-brewers add bittering hops to the copper as the wort is being collected, before the wort is boiled, asserting that this produces a better hop character than adding them later. I cannot see any real reason why this should be, but as I do not have any experience to the contrary, I will accept that it might be.

More common is to add bittering hops to the copper as the wort comes to the boil. This can cause more foaming and the risk of a sudden boilover, so it must be attended to carefully until the initial foaming has subsided, unless you are lucky enough to have an oversized boiler. It is, however, the most popular method.

The final method is to add the hops after the wort has been boiling for some time – 15 minutes or more – after proteins in the wort start to visibly clump together and fall out of suspension (known as the hot break). This gives better utilisation and reduces the tendency for a sudden boilover, but it extends the total boil time because the hops still need to be boiled for the full 90 minutes, or whatever the recipe calls for.

Whichever method is used, and it is really down to personal preference, it is important that the hops receive the full boil period. Indeed, the longer the boil the more mellow the hop bitterness becomes. That is not to say that it is any less bitter, slightly more bitter in fact, but any harshness in the bitterness diminishes with a longer boil.

Late hopping

Late hopping is the technique of adding hops for just the last five or ten minutes of the boil to add flavour and aroma. A quantity of the best aroma hops, typically equivalent to 25 per cent, but anywhere between 15 and 30 per cent of the total hops, is usually employed.

In theory at least, late hops do not contribute much bitterness to the brew because the short boiling period that they receive does not give enough time for much of the alpha acid bitterness to be extracted. However, late hops are rarely in the wort for the short period that the figure of five or ten minutes would seem at face value; they are often hanging around for 30 minutes to an hour until the wort is cooled and run off. There is plenty of time for some isomerisation to occur during this period, albeit at a lower rate due to the lower temperatures involved.

Individual equipment set-up and technique will also affect this. Emptying the copper straight after the boil and cooling in the collection vessel will extract less bitterness than cooling in the copper. Putting late hops in a bag and fishing them out after the prescribed time will also contribute less bitterness. Older hops will contribute more bitterness than fresher hops, no matter what, because oxidised beta acid is more readily soluble than alpha acid and does not require time for isomerisation.

The longer the late hops are boiled, the more the aroma components are driven off. The aroma components are driven off before the flavour components and by varying the boil time changes to the flavour profile can be achieved.

There is a school of thought among some commercial sources that all hops added for flavour purposes need a short, minimum boil time to drive off the undesirable volatiles, particularly with some of the modern hops.

Post-boil hopping

This is the technique of steeping some hops in the wort after it has been boiled. This, too, adds hop character. This time, high-quality aroma hops – between 10 and 15 per cent of the total – are steeped in the wort after the boil, after the temperature has dropped somewhat. Many home-brewers wait until the temperature has dropped to about 80°C before adding the hops. Because there is no boil and the temperature is lower, little bitterness is extracted, but aroma is extracted and less of the aroma volatiles are driven off.

Many commercial brewers use this technique in preference to late hopping because they use a domed, enclosed copper that operates under pressure – to add late hops would require opening the hatchway, which drops the pressure, and then the copper has to be returned to full pressure. It also fills the brewhouse with steam. It is much easier for them to put the hops onto the plates of their *hop back* (used to strain the wort) before the copper is emptied into it. In home-brewing we usually use a combined copper and hop back, and adding the hops directly to the copper after the boil has finished achieves the same thing.

Again, the likelihood that older hops may contribute some bitterness should be appreciated, because oxidised beta acid is available immediately and does not require the time for isomerisation that alpha acid does.

Hop tea

This is a technique that has been used by home-brewers since the revival of home-brewing in the 1960s, although it is not used much in real ale production these days. A hop tea is a quantity of hops infused in hot water for a period of around 30 minutes and added to the copper after the boil has finished.

Dry hopping

Dry hopping is the term used to describe the practice of adding a few hop cones to the cask after filling. This will add a hop aroma to the beer but does not add hop flavour or contribute to the bitterness. Only the best quality aroma-type hops should be used because some varieties of hop add a grassy flavour that some people dislike, and any objectionable volatiles do not have the opportunity to escape. Dry hopping is far more common in commercial beers than late hopping or post-boil hopping. Indeed, it is a centuries-old practice that was used by all the best pale ale brewers.

Using different varieties of hop

There will come a time when you want to use a different variety of bittering hop from the one specified in a recipe. This may be because the specified hops are not in stock at your usual supplier and you are forced to substitute, or simply because you wish to experiment or use up hops that you already have. Another reason could be that the alpha acid of the hops currently available is widely different from the ones specified, even though they are the same variety. Usually it is safe to ignore differences in alpha acid between hops of the same variety unless the differences are really large. The tolerances and variables within the brewing process will confound any attempts at achieving high accuracy.

Unfortunately, a direct weight-for-weight substitution of one hop for another will not provide the same level of bitterness, but a simple calculation will reveal the correct quantity to use. Assuming that you wish to maintain an equivalent level of bitterness, a simple comparison of the alpha acid ratios of the two hop varieties will provide the new quantity. For example, if your recipe calls for 40 grams of Challenger, but you wish to use Golding instead, the following simple relationship is all that is required:

$$\text{New weight of hops} = \frac{\text{Quantity of specified hops} \times \text{Alpha acid of specified hops}}{\text{Alpha acid of substitute hops}}$$

Assuming that Challenger has an alpha acid content of 7.6 per cent and that Golding has an alpha acid content of 5.7 per cent, the sum then becomes:

$$\text{New weight of hops} = \frac{40 \times 7.6}{5.7} = 53 \text{ grams}$$

The same method applies when compensating for widely differing alpha acid levels between the same variety of hop. This formula is only applicable to primary bittering hops. Aroma or late hops are not affected by alpha acid, but by essential oils. It is not really appropriate to attempt to compensate for aroma between varieties because different varieties have widely different aroma characteristics and flavours anyway, and are not comparable. However, if you are using the same variety of aroma hop as specified in the recipe, and its alpha acid is widely different from the figure specified in the table below, it is fair to assume that the essential oil will also differ in the same ratio as the alpha acid. The formula above can be safely used to adjust the quantity of aroma or late hops used, using alpha acid as the basis.

The typical alpha acid content of the most common varieties of hops are listed below, including all the hops specified in the recipes in this book. The recipes are normalised to the alpha acid values specified in this table.

HOP ALPHA ACID

VARIETY	ALPHA-ACID	SOURCE	TYPE
Admiral	14.6%	England	Bittering
Amarillo	5.0%	USA	Aroma
Bodicea hops	7.9%	England	Dual purpose
Bramling Cross	6.3%	England	Aroma
Brewers gold	6.1%	Germany	Aroma
Cascade	5.4%	USA	Aroma
Challenger	7.6%	England	Dual purpose
First Gold	8.3%	England	Dual purpose
Fuggle	4.9%	England	Aroma
Golding	5.7%	England	Aroma
Herald	12.7%	England	Bittering
Hersbrucker	2.9%	Germany	Aroma
Liberty	4.5%	USA	Aroma
Mittlefruh	4.3%	Germany	Aroma
Mount Hood	4.4%	USA	Aroma
Northdown	8.3%	England	Dual purpose
Northern Brewer	8.2%	Germany	Dual purpose
Perle	6.3%	Germany	Dual purpose
Phoenix	11.5%	England	Bittering
Pilgrim	11.6%	England	Bittering
Pioneer	9.0%	England	Bittering
Progress	6.4%	England	Aroma
Saaz	3.3%	Czech Republic	Aroma
Soverign	5.7%	England	Aroma
Styrian Golding	4.5%	Slovenia	Aroma
Target	11.4%	England	Bittering
Whitbread Golding	6.4%	England	Aroma
Williamete	4.7%	USA	Aroma

Bitterness Units

A bitterness unit is the magic number that provides a universal method of mathematically quantifying the bitterness of beer. In Europe we call them European Bitterness Units (EBUs). They are also called International Bitterness Units (IBUs). The amount of iso-alpha acid in a beer can be measured analytically and this is reduced to a number that represents a scale of bitterness. That scale is directly related to the quantity of hops in a beer. The bitterness of a beer in EBUs is given by:

$$EBU = \frac{\text{weight of hops x alpha acid\% x utilisation\%}}{\text{volume brewed x 10}}$$

To find the weight of hops required to produce a given bitterness in a given volume of beer the formula can be rewritten thus:

$$\text{Weight of hops} = \frac{\text{EBU x 10 x volume brewed}}{\text{alpha acid\% x utilisation\%}}$$

Where:
Volume brewed is in litres
Weight of hops is in grams
Alpha acid of hops is in per cent
Hop utilisation is in per cent

It should be appreciated that the formula deals only with the bitterness contributed by alpha acid. The bitterness, if any, contributed by beta acid is ignored. Different analytical techniques give different values of alpha acid for the same beer and perceived bitterness is not the same as measured or calculated bitterness. Working backwards from EBUs to determine the quantity of hops is not really feasible without a knowledge of personal utilisation efficiency.

Hop utilisation

This brings us neatly to the complicated and rather poorly defined subject of hop utilisation. Although a given variety of hop might contain, say, five per cent alpha acid, we only manage to extract, or isomerise, a small fraction of that. The amount of alpha acid we manage to get from the hop, compared with the total alpha acid contained within the hop, is known as hop utilisation and is again expressed in per cent. It represents hop extraction efficiency. Actual hop utilisation is surprisingly low: somewhere between 20 and 35 per cent depending upon conditions – often much lower.

Utilisation is another thorn in the side of home-brewers because it is extremely variable and affected by just about everything. It is probably obvious that the length of time that hops are boiled affects utilisation, but less obvious is that the specific gravity of the wort, the vigour of the boil, boiler geometry, hop rate, whether the boiler is covered or open, and even barometric pressure will also affect it. Different brewing methods and different equipment can exhibit quite large differences.

Hop utilisation is also highly recipe dependent. The variables are so many that hop utilisation simply cannot be calculated. Generally a home-brewer derives a figure for hop utilisation empirically, by trial and error.

For most of us it is simpler to use a single figure for hop utilisation irrespective of other influences, particularly if the majority of beers are within a small original gravity range. The idea is to use the same figure for utilisation for the initial brews, irrespective of the type of beer being brewed. If the beers are consistently too bitter, the utilisation factor is increased next time; if it consistently too low, the utilisation factor is reduced. Within a few brews a figure will be derived that suits the system.

If we assume a figure of 25 per cent is used for utilisation, to achieve 30 units of bitterness in 23 litres of beer using Golding hops at an alpha acid content of 5.7 per cent and a utilisation of 25 per cent gives:

Weight of hops =
$$\frac{30 \times 10 \times 23}{5.7 \times 25} = 48 \text{ grams}$$

This assumes a minimum of 90-minutes vigorous boil. There are theoretical objections to using a fixed utilisation factor for all beers, but it is probably as accurate in the long run as any of the more complicated methods.

However, one of the greatest influences on hop utilisation is the amount of protein in the wort during

HOP UTILISATION FACTOR VS ORIGINAL GRAVITY

Original gravity is in degrees gravity, hop utilisation is in per cent

OG	%	OG	%
1030	28.8	1070	20.6
1031	28.6	1071	20.4
1032	28.4	1072	20.2
1033	28.2	1073	20.0
1034	28.0	1074	19.8
1035	27.8	1075	19.6
1036	27.6	1076	19.4
1037	27.4	1077	19.1
1038	27.2	1078	18.9
1039	27.0	1079	18.7
1040	26.8	1080	18.5
1041	26.6	1081	18.3
1042	26.4	1082	18.1
1043	26.1	1083	17.9
1044	25.9	1084	17.7
1045	25.7	1085	17.3
1046	25.5	1086	17.3
1047	25.3	1087	17.1
1048	25.1	1088	16.9
1049	24.9	1089	16.7
1050	24.7	1090	16.5
1051	24.5	1091	16.3
1052	24.3	1092	16.1
1053	24.1	1093	15.9
1054	23.0	1094	15.6
1055	23.7	1095	15.2
1056	23.5	1096	15.2
1057	23.3	1097	15.0
1058	23.1	1098	14.8
1059	22.9	1099	14.6
1060	22.6	1100	14.4
1061	22.4	1101	14.2
1062	22.2	1102	14.0
1063	22.0	1103	13.8
1064	21.8	1104	13.6
1065	21.6	1105	13.2
1066	21.4	1106	13.2
1067	21.2	1107	13.0
1068	21.0	1108	12.8
1069	20.8	1109	12.6

the boil. The protein has the effect of absorbing bittering substances and dragging them out of solution with the trub (sediment). Hop utilisation is inversely proportional to the amount of protein in the wort, among other things. Different beers, particularly beers of different strength, will have differing amounts of protein and thus different hop utilisations.

Only primary malts, that is enzymic malts, contain protein. Crystal malt, highly-coloured malts and sugar do not contribute protein. As the majority of a grist (crushed malt for mashing) – at least 80 per cent – is made up of primary enzymic malts, an approximation for wort protein can be determined from the specific gravity of the wort. Technically, the weight of the enzymic malts and the sum of their typical protein contents should be used to come up with a figure, but it is much more complicated and probably no more accurate than basing the figure on specific gravity.

For the sake of simplicity, the recipes in this book use original gravity as the basis to estimate hop utilisation according to the table on *p23*. Any bitterness contributed by late hops or post-boil hops is ignored.

Storing hops

Hops are not very stable and must be stored carefully if the quality of the hop is to be maintained. Hops can oxidise very quickly during storage and they are also photosensitive. Hop merchants keep their hops in cold store under carefully controlled conditions, just above freezing point, which enables them to remain in good condition for several years.

The photosensitivity of hops is an important degradation factor. Hops are harvested and are at their best just before they fully ripen. Exposing hops to sunlight, or any source of light at the correct wavelength, will cause the ripening process to continue and degrade the hop. The great breweries of old took great pains to ensure that the hops were never exposed to direct sunlight, even while they were waiting to go into the copper. The copper-rooms of breweries were often equipped with large canopies under which the hops were held in readiness for the copper, which shielded them from sunlight coming through the roof lights. This photosensitivity is carried through to the finished beer.

The reason for beer being traditionally supplied in dark bottles is to prevent the beer from becoming sun-struck. A sun-struck beer has unpleasant off-flavours. Exposure to fluorescent lights can cause hop degradation or a sun-struck beer in a short time.

When storing hops at home, they can by placed in tightly closed polythene bags so that they are airtight and kept in the coolest place you can find. Many home-brewers store their hops in the freezer quite satisfactorily. It should be remembered, however, that commercial hop merchants take care to ensure that their hops are maintained at a temperature just above freezing during cold storage. Most traditional brewers keep their hops at a cool ambient temperature in their hop store.

Yeast

There are not many life forms simpler than the humble yeast cell. It is a mere fungus or mould, yet it has probably provided some of the greatest services to mankind, and given more pleasure to the human race than almost anything else.

In the days when water supplies were unsafe, yeast supplied us with safe and wholesome fluids to drink in the form of ale and wine and helped to make a cheap and nourishing food in the form of bread, to fill the hungry bellies of the people. At one time, ale and bread were considered to be the two major necessities of life – the staple diet of the populace. Yeast was responsible for both.

Brewer's yeast is a rich source of B-complex vitamins and ends up in all sorts of foods and numerous vitamin supplements. Yeast can be used genetically to manufacture a number of medicines and antibodies. Indeed, one of its kin, a fungus called *penicillium notatum*, was responsible for the foundation of modern antibiotics, due its ability to generate bactericides that kill susceptible forms of bacteria, or at least inhibit their growth. Alas, there are no monuments erected to celebrate the part that the humble yeast has played in the development of mankind.

A minor miracle

Although we all know that yeast is responsible for the production of alcohol, if we are to have trouble-free brewing it is important to know a little bit about the conditions that yeast requires in order to produce this minor miracle.

When yeast is first added to the wort it needs to grow at a fast rate in order to establish itself and form the protective yeast head. In order to be able to do this it needs plenty of dissolved air in the wort, because yeast can only multiply significantly under aerobic conditions – in the presence of dissolved air. It is important that at the time the yeast is *pitched* (added to the wort) the wort is well aerated. When the yeast has multiplied sufficiently, and in the course of doing so has used up all the dissolved air in the wort, it is forced to respire anaerobically – without air – and it begins to produce alcohol. It is only under anaerobic conditions that yeast produces alcohol.

Types of yeast

There are a great many varieties of yeast used in brewing, but they all fit into one of two broad classifications: bottom working and top working. Bottom working yeasts, these days simply called lager yeasts, are those where most of the yeast settles to the bottom of the vessel during fermentation. The major characteristic of this type of yeast is that it will work at much lower temperatures than its top-working counterpart. It is used for Pilsner-style lagers. Top-working yeasts are those where most of the yeast rises to the surface of the wort after fermentation. This is the type of yeast used in traditional British-style beers.

However, just because a yeast head forms on a fermenting beer it does not mean that it is a true top worker. Often this is simply yeast carried to the surface by the carbon dioxide produced during fermentation. The top-working characteristic of a yeast is also dependent upon the conditions in which it is working, temperature in particular, and on the composition of the media in which it finds itself. The flocculation characteristics of yeast are particularly sensitive to environment, which is one reason why most commercially packaged yeast loses its top-working ability.

North/South divide

Top-working English ale yeast can be further classified into two broad sub-divisions which I have termed 'Northern yeast' and 'Southern yeast', although the geographical distinction is not so apparent these days.

Northern yeast, sometimes referred to as slow or aerobic yeast, is common in the north of England, Yorkshire in particular, but can also be found in other areas. Without going too deeply into technicalities, Northern yeast does not particularly enjoy making alcohol and needs frequent rousing to maintain fermentation – every few hours the yeast head needs to be stirred back into the wort and aerated. As a consequence it produces copious amounts of surplus yeast. A special fermentation vessel known as a Yorkshire Square, now almost extinct, evolved to cope with this style of yeast. A Yorkshire Square needed attention every two or three hours. Modern breweries that use Northern yeast keep the yeast active by pumping the wort from the bottom of the fermentation vessel and spraying it back in at the top, for about 15 minutes every couple of hours. This keeps the wort circulating through the yeast head, effectively the job of the Yorkshire Square.

You cannot get much further south than Ringwood, in Hampshire, but Ringwood Brewery yeast is, in fact, a Northern yeast. It originated from the now defunct Hull Brewery. Despite its craving for attention, it is quite a popular yeast with home-brewers. It is available packaged from home-brewing shops, although the packaged version is not as good as the real stuff that comes out of the brewery. Northern yeast when used in home-brewing is usually roused twice a day, once in the morning and once at night, for the duration of the fermentation period, and that works well. The brewer, after all, cannot be nursing his yeast 24 hours a day.

Southern yeast, commonly used in the south of England, also known as fast or anaerobic yeast, is less demanding and will sit and do its thing unattended, although an occasional rousing is sometimes required.

Packaged yeast

Packaged yeast purchased from your local home-brewing shop is the easiest and most convenient way of obtaining yeast. I am sure that the suppliers do try to give us good-quality yeast but, nevertheless, most packaged yeast leaves a lot to be desired and does not behave true to type when compared to the real thing from the donor brewery. The dried varieties in particular give an unremarkable but accelerated fermentation – usually with no skimmable head, even though many of them are described as 'ale yeast' or 'top fermenting' – and a dry beer lacking in any yeast character. Liquid yeast suspensions should, in theory, be much better, but in practice even they do not live up to expectations.

The problem with most packaged yeast is that the propagation and drying processes change the character of the yeast somewhat. Dried yeast is grown in commercial propagators on low-gravity sucrose, continuously injected with high concentrations of oxygen, and special reactor techniques are used to achieve the high biomass necessary for the drying stage; in short it is aerobically force grown. High oxygen concentration is maintained to produce sterols, lipids and fatty acids which condition the cell walls and provide energy reserves. These energy reserves enable the yeast to go to work and grow almost as soon as it is pitched in the wort without the need for initial aeration, and is the reason why most dried yeast shows activity sooner than other types.

In contrast, brewer's yeast has adapted to maltose as its energy source, at higher gravities than the typical propagator employs, and low concentrations of dissolved air (not high concentrations of pure oxygen). In a brewery environment the yeast builds its sterols during the aerobic growth phase using dissolved air, has an anaerobic phase during which it produces alcohol, and rises to the surface when fermentation is complete to be skimmed off for reuse. For centuries brewers have been skimming yeast from the top of the fermentation vessel to use to inoculate the next batch.

Deviation from these conditions places the yeast under stress, and it modifies itself to compensate, which in itself forces genetic drift. Even slightly different nutrients cause the cell shape to change. Some yeasts do not perform well without hop components being present, and others do not perform properly without copper ions being present – the result of centuries of brewing vessels being fabricated from, or lined with, copper.

The most obvious change to the brewer is that commercially

propagated yeast loses its top-working characteristic and often the characteristic flavours associated with top-working beers.

Dried yeast

Notwithstanding all that I have said earlier, dried yeast is the most common way that home-brewers inoculate their wort. It is inexpensive, convenient, robust, easily obtainable, easy to use, has a long shelf life and does not necessarily require a starter culture. However, a starter is regarded as beneficial by many home-brewers, particularly if the yeast is not particularly new. Some brewers merely sprinkle dried yeast on the surface of their cooled wort and achieve satisfactory results, but rehydrating the yeast, as described on *p32*, is the generally recommended procedure in lieu of a starter and only takes a few minutes.

There are just a few types of dried yeast currently available: Safale-S04 will not win any prizes for flavour and is not a proper top-worker, but it ferments well and fast, sediments easily, produces beers of good clarity, and packs down tightly onto the bottom of bottles, making it a good choice for bottled beers. It is an excellent yeast for beginners because it is novice proof as long as careful attention is paid to the temperatures of rehydrating and pitching into the wort, which should be between 20°C and 30°C in both cases.

Danstar Windsor is another popular yeast because it has a better flavour profile than S04. It has excellent clarity, but does not stick so well as S04 to the bottom of bottles. It is preferred over S04 by some home-brewers because of the flavour characteristics imparted to the beer.

Dried yeast should be stored in a refrigerator or freezer until ready for use, to prolong shelf life. Allow the yeast to acclimatise to ambient temperature before rehydrating. Try to avoid subjecting the yeast to sudden temperature shocks.

Liquid yeast

Liquid yeast – yeast in a liquid suspension – is a superior product to dried yeast in terms of authenticity of type and flavour. It is, however, more difficult to use and more expensive. The major advantages are that because it is easier to produce, there is a much wider range of different liquid yeast strains available, and because it is not grown to achieve high biomasses prior to drying and is not subjected to the stresses of drying, it can retain more of its true characteristics.

Liquid yeast is available in two forms. In its simplest and cheapest form it is simply a vial or tube containing a quantity of yeast cells in a liquid suspension medium. These vials contain an insufficient quantity to pitch directly into the wort and must be propagated up to a sufficient quantity in a starter medium, as described on *p32*.

The second form is known as 'smack-pack'. This is a twin-sachet arrangement; the inner sachet contains a nutrient medium and the outer contains the yeast in isolation. The idea is that a few hours before brewing, you give the sealed package a smack in the palm of the hand, which ruptures the inner sachet and releases the nutrient into the outer package to mix with the yeast. The yeast then begins to work and the package swells as CO_2 is produced. When you are ready to pitch the yeast, the package is opened and tipped into the wort. Smack-packs are claimed to contain sufficient yeast to pitch directly into the wort, but unless the yeast is very fresh I would not risk it without a starter.

It should be remembered that many of these yeasts are of American origin and have been transported halfway round the world, presumably having been left hanging around in various warehouses en-route under less than ideal conditions, before traversing down the supply chain in Britain. The viability is bound to be less than optimum by the time they are opened.

White Labs' WLP023 Burton Ale yeast is a popular liquid yeast and is a good one to begin with if you are experimenting for the first time. It imparts the characteristic Burton flavour, clears down well and sticks to the bottom of bottles; an excellent general-purpose yeast.

Liquid yeasts must be stored in a refrigerator but not frozen, and will keep for about six months.

Yeast slopes

Yeast slopes, or slants, are another way of obtaining yeast. These are phials of yeast supplied on a solidified wort-based medium. In my view these are far superior to most liquid yeasts because the yeast is grown under conditions that imitate true brewery conditions. The wort-based solid medium on which it is supplied keeps the yeast happy during transit and storage. My experience of yeast slopes is that they do behave as true-to-type brewery yeast when cultured up, and I would always use them in preference to other liquid types. They are also a bit cheaper to buy than most liquid types.

The best known yeast slopes are the Brewlab slopes that are produced by the University of Sunderland and are sold by good home-brewing shops. Brewlab slopes are available in more than a dozen varieties covering the major geographic brewing areas of Britain, and others are available to special order.

Yeast slopes require a starter to be made up before use. A 300 ml starter is made up as described on *p32*, and when the starter has cooled to room temperature a small amount is poured into the slope phial, the cap replaced and the phial is given a good shake to loosen the yeast from the slope, left to stand for a few minutes and then given another shake and poured into the main bulk of the starter.

Do not be put off by the apparently low quantity of yeast cells contained on these slopes. The yeast is highly viable and raring to go. In fact, in my experience these culture-up much faster and more reliably than liquid yeasts I have used in the past.

Live brewer's yeast

Many areas of Britain have a micro-brewery nearby these days, and if you are lucky it will sell you real live brewer's yeast. Once you have used proper top-working live ex-brewery yeast you won't want to use anything else.

You may have to take your own container to the micro for it to fill. A domestic vacuum-flask is ideal – it will keep the yeast at a constant temperature until you get it home. Disinfect the flask first as a precaution.

Wort aeration

The boiling phase of beer production drives off any dissolved air that may be present. It is therefore necessary for us to aerate the wort after it has cooled. Wort aeration is important to give the yeast the oxygen it needs during its formative hours to build up its energy reserves and multiply sufficiently to do some useful work.

The usual way to do this is to pour the cooled wort slowly from one fermentation bin to another a couple of times, or run the wort slowly from bin to bin through the fitted tap, ensuring that there is plenty of splashing and turbulence. This can get a fair amount of air into solution, but is not practical if you need to aerate part-way through fermentation, which some yeasts require.

Vigorous stirring with a brewer's paddle or a long-handled spoon does a good job. The easiest way of doing this is to put the paddle into a cordless drill and use it to give the beer a good whisking. It will foam profusely, but simply wait for the foam to subside between bursts and repeat as often as necessary.

Some people aerate using an aquarium air pump and airstone, sometimes using a HEPA in-line filter to reduce the chance of bacterial infection. This is effective, and has the benefit of being perhaps more sterile than other methods.

It is important to cool the wort to pitching temperature before attempting to aerate, because the solubility of air and oxygen is too low at a high temperature. With some yeasts it may be necessary to rouse and aerate further during fermentation. When fermentation is over, or close to finishing, care should be taken to ensure air is kept out of the beer from that point onwards.

Rousing

Rousing entails stirring the yeast back into suspension. Some yeasts, such as Ringwood, require frequent rousing as well as aeration, and most yeasts will benefit from a rousing about 24 hours after pitching. If a brew slows, or stops fermenting early, a rousing will almost always get it into step again.

Have no fear about doing this – many home-brewers are overly worried about infection and oxidation and are afraid to do this sort of thing in case it upsets the beer, but the consequence of not doing it when it is necessary is a spoiled beer. As long as there is plenty of fermentable material remaining in the beer, it is safe to rouse. If the beer is at, or close to, the expected final gravity, it is important to keep air out of the beer and it is not safe to rouse.

The disinfected brewer's paddle is a good way of rousing and aerating. If you are fermenting in an open fermenter, skim the top few millimetres of yeast from the surface to remove any airborne dust that may have settled on it, then give it a good whisking. Job done.

Yeast performance

A good, top-working English ale yeast should quickly establish itself into a thick, dense, rocky head. This head should be two or three inches deep, have a density of something like whipped cream, and look like something out of *Quatermass*. The term 'rocky head' is an attempt to convey the impression of a thick, ragged, uneven surface of chunky appearance as opposed to a weak, self-levelling foam. The appearance changes with differing conditions and during different stages of fermentation – indeed every head is different. However, the description gives you the general idea of things, and if you achieve something close to it, your yeast is performing well.

If you are using high-quality ingredients and a yeast starter solution and aerating your wort before, or just after, pitching the yeast, you will achieve good yeast performance. A further requirement of a good yeast is that it clears down quickly and unaided after casking. If you bottle your beers, a type of yeast that packs down firmly and adheres to the bottom of the bottle as a film is almost a necessity, otherwise it will be difficult to pour. Some yeasts collect as a loose clump at the bottom of the bottle and require more care when pouring.

Fermentation temperature

The fermentation temperature for an ale, using a proper ale yeast, should be between 18-22°C (the optimum temperature is 20°C). If you are fermenting in a shed or garage during winter when the ambient air temperature is low, a higher fermentation temperature may be beneficial; perhaps as high as 24°C. The trick is to maintain the lowest temperature at which the yeast functions properly. Too low a temperature and the yeast head may drop into the beer; too high a temperature and off-flavours may result. Thermostatically controlled fermentation heaters (based on aquarium heaters) are available in home-brew shops and fish-fanciers' shops. Insulation round the fermenter will help to prevent against temperature shocks when fermenting in a garage or shed.

In order to ensure that the yeast head is rapidly formed, it is beneficial to pitch the yeast when the wort temperature is relatively high, between 25-30°C, and allow the temperature to drop to a more appropriate fermentation temperature when the head has formed.

Yeast rehydration

Much home-brewing literature, particularly instructions supplied with beer kits, advocates simply sprinkling dried yeast on the surface of the wort to start fermentation. Many home-brewers use this method because it is the way they have always done it, with varying degrees of success.

You will get a faster and more reliable start if you rehydrate your yeast before pitching. The drill is to sprinkle the yeast onto the surface of a volume of boiled and cooled water equal to ten times its own weight at a temperature of around 30°C maximum – around 100 ml for a 10 gram packet. Cover and leave to stand for 15 minutes before stirring. Stand for a further 15 minutes and then whisk into a cream. When you are ready to pitch, mix with an equal volume of wort from your fermenter, stir and pitch.

Remove the packet from the fridge or freezer in ample time for the yeast to acclimatise to room temperature before rehydrating. If you have any doubts about the age

and viability of the yeast, it would be safer to make a yeast starter as described below.

Yeast starter culture

When using liquid yeast, recovered yeast or a dried yeast of small quantity or doubtful viability, it is essential to make a yeast starter solution before the brewing session. A starter solution ensures that your beer is supplied with an adequate quantity of active yeast that is able to establish itself rapidly and form a protective head before bacteria have a chance to gain a foothold.

A yeast starter culture takes only a few minutes to make up. Make it two or three days before you plan to brew and you can be sure that you have an adequate quantity of active yeast, grown under conditions of reasonable sterility, before starting. You can also be sure that the yeast is viable, active and bacteriologically sound before committing it to a 25-litre batch. This minimises the risk of later problems with yeast performance or infection. The lag phase – the time between pitching the yeast and something starting to happen – is reduced considerably because the yeast has grown to a suitable volume and is active before it is pitched.

It is important to ensure that a yeast starter does not inadvertently become a bacteria starter as well so it should be prepared under reasonably sterile conditions. A combination of chemical disinfection and heat is the easiest way to ensure a sterile medium. I use the old-fashioned glass, one-pint milk bottles as culturing flasks because they are designed to withstand boiling water and pasteurisation, and will accept a winemaker's airlock and rubber bung if necessary. Great care should be taken to ensure that the bottle is not stressed and broken by suddenly subjecting it to boiling malt extract. The procedure is straightforward:

1 *Disinfect the bottle, an airlock, a rubber bung and a small funnel using domestic bleach or a proprietary cleaner. After sterilisation rinse the items thoroughly. Gradually preheat the bottle with hot water of incremental temperature then fill it with boiling water and leave it to stand.*

2 *Bring approximately 300 ml of water to the boil in a saucepan then add about four tablespoons (55 grams) of malt extract, stirring continuously to avoid burning until it is properly dissolved. Simmer for 10 or 15 minutes then turn off the heat.*

3 *Carefully empty the hot water from the bottle and use the funnel to pour in the hot malt extract solution. Loosely cover the mouth of the bottle with a piece of aluminium kitchen foil, allow to cool for a while, then stand it in a bowl of cold water until it has cooled to room temperature. The solution will cool faster if the bottle is given a shake from time to time to re-mix the contents, but take care not to scald yourself.*

4 *When the solution has cooled to room temperature and with the foil still covering the neck of the bottle, give it a vigorous shake to admit oxygen into the solution.*

5 *Add the yeast, give the bottle a final vigorous shake, fit the bung and airlock, or cover the mouth with a square of sterilised kitchen foil or sterile cotton-wool, and stand the starter in a warmish place at about 20°C. Ensure that the outside of the bottle is clean and free from malt extract solution as this will be a potential bug trap.*

6 *Regularly give the starter a shake to re-aerate it and encourage further yeast growth.*

The yeast has grown to maximum volume and used up all its nutrients when CO_2 is no longer being generated. Regular re-aeration, say two or three times a day, will encourage the yeast to grow to a greater volume. This is not easy to do once growth has started, because shaking the bottle will cause any CO_2 in solution to be expelled rapidly and everything in the room will be covered with starter. If an airlock is used, temporarily remove it and replace with sterilised foil for the shaking.

Do not brew your main batch of beer until you are sure that the yeast is actively fermenting or has finished fermenting. The time taken for the starter to become sufficiently active for pitching is dependent upon yeast viability, initial quantity of yeast and temperature. If you intend to brew on a Sunday morning you would probably make your yeast starter on a Thursday night; it can be kept under airlock for a few days until you are ready to brew. Give the starter a sniff before using it to ensure that it smells okay and is therefore likely to be infection free. You can even taste it once you have got to know what a healthy starter tastes like.

Recovering yeast from a bottled beer

The ability to recover yeast from a bottled beer is a useful way to obtain obscure yeasts, or yeasts appropriate to a particular beer. Most British bottled beers are filtered or pasteurised these days which removes or kills the yeast. However, some breweries produce a live, bottle-conditioned beer, and there are an increasing number of imported speciality beers that are unpasteurised. English home-brewers have traditionally used yeast kidnapped from a Guinness bottle, but live, bottle-conditioned Guinness has now been withdrawn, which is a shame: Guinness yeast is a great performer in almost any type of beer.

Even though a beer may be bottle conditioned, it does not mean that the yeast it contains is live. A number of breweries bottle condition their beer, but when it has conditioned 'far enough', they shove the bottles through a tunnel-pasteuriser thereby killing the yeast and stabilising the beer.

Breweries' bottle conditioned beer ranges change all the time, but suitable candidates for likely success can be selected from CAMRA's *Good Bottled Beer Guide*.

The procedure for propagating yeast from a bottled beer is quite simple:

1 Give the donor bottle a wipe down with your standard disinfectant and stand it in a cool place. Leave it undisturbed for a day or two to allow the yeast to settle to the bottom.

2 Make up a yeast starter solution using the procedure described above.

3 When the starter has cooled to room temperature, carefully uncap the donor bottle and decant all but the last half-inch of the contents into a glass, taking care to ensure that any yeast sediment is left behind in the bottle.

4 Give the remaining contents of the donor bottle a good shake in order to dislodge any yeast clinging to the bottom of the bottle. Tip the entire contents, dregs and all, into the yeast starter solution.

5 Drink contents of glass.

Ensure that the donor beer is as fresh as possible. Some commercial beers have a very low residual yeast count and it may take a couple of days or even longer for signs of activity to show in the starter medium. Some types of yeast pack firmly down on to the bottom of the bottle. With these it may be necessary to pour the solution from the starter into the donor bottle, shake and pour back into the starter repeatedly until the yeast has been dislodged.

It is regarded as good practice to flame the mouths of the bottles immediately before transfer of the fluids. This entails giving the whole rim a lick of flame with a gas-lighter, usually the sort of thing used for lighting gas stoves or gas-powered barbecues. This burns off any bacteria lurking there.

Propagating yeast

When they have found a yeast that suits them, many home-brewers want to continue using it. If your favourite yeast happens to be a packaged yeast there is no problem but if your yeast is from a commercial brewery or from some other obscure source, you will need to propagate the strain yourself. Propagation has the advantage of adapting the yeast to perform well in your own particular style of beer. Another advantage is that the yeast supply is of known performance and origin, and free from change imposed by commercial packagers.

Although it is possible to recover yeast from the fermentation vessel and store it in a refrigerator (2-5°C) for up to about a week, refrigeration or freezing is not really suitable for long-term storage of yeast collected in this way. The easiest and best way of propagating yeast is to recover it from your own bottled beers. Even if you usually cask your ales, there is no hardship in filling a couple of bottles from the cask and storing them. You could even brew a special batch of beer and bottle it for propagation purposes. These bottles can be stored away in the back of the garage somewhere and brought out on special occasions or for yeast recovery.

The best type of beer for propagation purposes is a strongish, all-malt, hoppy brew of around OG 1040-1060. The high alcohol and hop content of such a brew will help to keep the beer sound and infecting bacteria in their place.

Take extra care over sterilisation and cleanliness for this particular brew. If the beer goes off in storage you cannot reuse the yeast. Use brews bottled during the winter, when infection is much less likely. After the bottles have been filled and capped, wipe them with a disinfectant such as household bleach to remove any traces of spilt beer. Yeast is recovered from the bottles using the technique described above.

Clarification Aids

Clarification aids and other additives are not strictly ingredients because they do not stay in the beer or contribute directly to its flavour. Additives generally control brewing processes in one way or another to improve the taste, appearance or shelf life of the beer. The most common of these are fining agents which help with clarity and polish. These pass through the beer and settle out, and thus do not really qualify as ingredients.

Copper finings

Copper finings, as the name suggests, are added to the copper during the latter part of the boil to assist in the coagulation of protein, helping it to settle out as trub. If excessive protein remains in the wort it will cause a haze in the finished beer. Although satisfactory clarity may be obtained without recourse to copper finings, a haze due to protein is one of those things that only becomes apparent when it is too late to do anything about it. For pale ales it is standard practice, even in commercial breweries, to add copper finings during the last few minutes of the boil.

Irish moss

Irish moss is the traditional form of copper finings. It is derived from *chondrus crispus*, a seaweed found on the Atlantic coastlines of northern Europe and north America. It is abundant on the rocky Irish

west coast, which probably accounts for its name, but it can be found on the west coast of Britain too. It is a charge-based fining system in which the negatively-charged molecules of Irish moss attract positively charged protein molecules, which form larger, heavier flocs which then settle out.

Irish moss is used at about 100 mg per litre, which works out at 2.5 grams for a 23-litre batch. It is important not to overdo the dose, although the application has to be grossly overdone for it to cause a problem.

Irish moss is available in various forms, or at least in various grain sizes, ranging from a fine powder to something resembling granules, and also in flakes. I will leave you to work out what 2.5 grams of Irish moss looks like, but most people just chuck a teaspoonful into the boiler 10 or 15 minutes before the end of the boil.

Protofloc

Protofloc is a concentrated seaweed-based copper finings extracted from a blend of seaweeds using an alkali extraction process. It is supplied in both powder and tablet form and is used in the same way as Irish moss, added to the boiler about ten minutes before the end of the boil. It is more concentrated than raw Irish moss and about a quarter of the amount is required to achieve the same ends – 0.75 grams for a 23-litre batch. Protofloc tablets are easier to use because it is easier to divide a tablet than it is to weigh a small quantity of powder. A half or even a third of a Protofloc tablet is sufficient for 23 litres of beer.

Whirlfloc

Whirlfloc is a similar product to Protofloc. Whirlfloc is used at 20 to 60 mg per litre, which is about one gram for a 23-litre batch. A Whirlfloc tablet weighs 2.5 grams, so half a Whirlfloc tablet is sufficient for 23 litres.

Beer fining

This is the act of removing yeast and some other bits and bobs from finished beer. Finings are usually added to the cask after the beer has matured for a while, particularly if auxiliary finings have been used beforehand.

It has to be said that most beers using a good yeast will clear down without fining, given time. The main reason for fining is to speed up the clearing process or to deal with

difficult yeast. It is not normal to fine beers destined for bottling because the yeast needs to pack down firmly on the bottom of the bottle, whereas fined beers tend to have 'fluffy bottoms' which makes the beer difficult to pour without disturbing the yeast and clouding the beer.

Isinglass or gelatine can be used as a fining agent. Isinglass is the superior product when fresh, and is the stuff that commercial breweries use.

Isinglass finings

And so on to the vexing subject of isinglass. Many home-brewers have problems with isinglass which, in home-brewing, is complicated by various issues, namely poor shelf life and highly optimistic instructions.

Isinglass is made from the swim bladders of certain fish, usually of the sturgeon variety. It is added during maturation in cask to assist in dragging yeast out of suspension thereby improving clarity. Isinglass is another charge-based fining system, only this time it has a positive charge that attracts negatively-charged particles, mostly yeast. It is the stuff that commercial brewers use.

Liquid isinglass has a shelf life of just four to eight weeks, and only then if the temperature is maintained below 15°C. At temperatures above 20°C it rapidly denatures and becomes ineffective. It takes a considerable act of faith to trust the ready-for-use finings from the home-brewing supply chain, because there is no guarantee that stringent storage and transport conditions have been met. However, if you can assure yourself that the liquid is fresh and has been stored properly, ready-for-use liquid finings will probably be the superior product. Get it home and into your refrigerator quickly.

Apart from the liquid varieties, there are various forms of dried isinglass available through the home-brew trade, but most of these are hampered by over-optimistic instructions. It will take days to make up good quality finings, not minutes as is often advocated on the packaging, and requires the use of a high-speed vortexing mixer to get the stuff to go into solution. There is one exception however – pre-hydrolysed isinglass powder. If the stuff in your packet looks like a fine powder and the word 'hydrolysed' is written on the packet somewhere, then you have a relatively easy time ahead of you. The isinglass has been pre-hydrolysed and freeze-dried, and is the closest you will get to instant finings, apart from the ready-for-use liquid.

Pre-hydrolysed isinglass is usually used at six grams per litre. Mix with water of low alkalinity. This can be achieved by boiling the water in a saucepan for 15-20 minutes, then racking it off the chalk sediment when cool. Alternatively use deionised water. Cool the water to below 16°C before use.

Add the powder to the water, 1.5 grams for 250 ml, and mix for two minutes with a blender. Allow to stand for 20 minutes, then give it another two minutes' blitz with the blender. It is then ready for use. It is probably better to make up the finings a day or so in advance, so keep the solution in the fridge and give it another blitz with the blender before use.

Harris Beer Brite is a pre-hydrolysed powder and, refreshingly for the world of isinglass, you can more or less trust the instructions on the packet. Beer Brite contains ingredients other than isinglass including silica hydrogel which absorbs chill-haze-causing proteins. You will need to use the whole packet for a 23-litre batch.

Isinglass usage

Isinglass finings, whether bought ready for use or made up yourself, are used at a rate of between 8 and 20 ml per litre of beer. That works out at between 200-500 ml of finings for 23-25 litres of beer. Pre-mix with a little beer, about the same amount as the finings, before gently adding to the cask. Stir gently, taking care not to introduce any significant amount of air into the beer.

The lower the temperature of the beer, the greater the fining action will be. If the beer is chilled sufficiently to throw a chill-haze before adding the finings, a substantial amount of the chill haze component will also be removed, giving a more stable beer.

If your beer does not have the clarity you expect, and if you can be sure that it is due to yeast in suspension and not some other cause, then increase the amount of finings for future brews.

Gelatine

Gelatine is the traditional fining agent used by home-brewers. It is not as efficient as isinglass, but it is a lot less hassle to make up and a lot cheaper. It relies on its inherent 'stickiness' to perform its fining action. Packets of gelatine are available in supermarkets. One sachet of unflavoured gelatine is enough to treat 23 litres of beer. If it is supplied loose, use 15 grams for 23 litres.

Making it up is simplicity itself. Empty the sachet or put 15 grams of gelatine into a mug and add a tablespoonful (about 20 ml) of cold water. Leave to stand for ten minutes to allow the gelatine to absorb the water, just like rehydrating yeast.

Boil some water and allow it to cool slightly – 85°C is about right – and add sufficient to bring the volume up to about 100 ml. Stir well until the gelatine has dissolved. Cover the mug with a saucer and allow to stand for at least ten minutes.

Never add boiling water directly to gelatine as it will denature it. Hot water helps the gelatine to dissolve and provides a pasteurisation function, hence the standing period. The water needs to be hot enough to facilitate the pasteurisation process, such that the temperature after mixing is about 75°C. There is no need to mess around with a thermometer – guesswork is good enough.

Once the temperature has dropped to below about 55°C it is safe to add it to the beer. Gently premix it with about 250 ml of your beer then stir it into the cask.

Auxiliary finings

Auxiliary finings are optional post-fermentation finings that are used in conjunction with isinglass finings to produce brilliant clarity in cask-conditioned beers, but they must not be added at the same time as isinglass. Auxiliary finings make particles in the beer negatively charged, thus when isinglass (which is positively charged) is added, all the particles are attracted to it, becoming heavy enough to drop out of suspension.

Auxiliary finings are added post fermentation, usually to the cask at the time of filling. They must not be added at the same time as isinglass finings because their charges will cancel each other out, making them both ineffective. The finings should be added at least 24 hours before isinglass finings. Auxiliary finings are usually added at a rate of two ml per litre, which amounts to 50 ml per 23 litre batch, which is at least easy to measure.

Water Treatment

So, the old water chestnut raises its ugly head. Water treatment is a complex subject for anyone unfamiliar with the basic chemistry involved and it is very difficult to convey those complexities in a collection of easily understood words. It is also true to say that a considerable amount of rubbish is spouted about water treatment, particularly on the Internet.

The truth is that water treatment is not as difficult or as important as some people make out. If you are a beginner, it is certainly not worth losing too much sleep over. See how your beer turns out before getting to grips with water treatment. It should be remembered that breweries all over the country were making perfectly satisfactory ales 200 years ago – long before water treatment was ever thought of.

Water treatment is a 20th-century phenomenon. However, Britain earned its reputation for excellent beer quality during the 18th and 19th centuries, when it was exported all over the world. At that time commercial brewers boiled their water before brewing, which would have reduced excessive chalk, but that was all in the way of water treatment.

It is probably true to say that in order to duplicate a particular brewer's beer, you will need to duplicate his water supply, but it is also true that most water supplies around Britain will produce acceptable beers without treatment. However, some minerals in water are detrimental to beer whereas others are beneficial. Therefore, a certain amount of water treatment will probably make an improvement.

There are two main reasons for water treatment and both are quite easy to achieve. The first is to adjust the acidity (pH) of the mash to be within an efficient range. The mash performs best when its acidity or pH is at 5.3, which is the optimum, but anywhere between 5.1 and 5.5 will give good performance. You can monitor your mash pH and thus your water treatment very easily by using simple, inexpensive narrow-range indicator papers available from your home-brew shop, but no beer is likely to fail completely if the mash pH happens to be somewhere else. The second reason is to provide an abundance of calcium. All of the brewing processes from mash reactions down to the clarity of the final beer need calcium as a co-enzyme in order to function properly. Everything will benefit from the presence of calcium (and a low pH). Mash reactions, hop extraction, trub formation, keeping qualities, yeast flocculation and clarity will all be improved.

Sources of water

All of our water comes to us in the form of rain. As it falls to earth it picks up quantities of atmospheric gases and pollutants that acidify it slightly. The most significant of these acids is carbonic acid which is produced by the admission of atmospheric carbon dioxide gas into solution. The acidified rainwater falls to earth, drains through the topsoil, percolates through mineral substrata and porous rock below the soil, through cracks and fissures in non-porous rock, and finally it settles onto a table of impervious rock where it waits to be collected. Alternatively, it may overflow into a river or surface as a spring.

On its journey through the earth the water absorbs mineral salts. The type and quantity of the salts is dependent on the type of rock through which the water passes before being collected. Rainwater that falls onto sedimentary rocks will absorb minerals on its journey through the earth. Some of these minerals are directly soluble in water, whereas others need to react with the carbonic acid picked up from the atmosphere to cause a chemical change in order to effect solubility. If the minerals dissolved in the water are substances such as salts of calcium or magnesium, we say the water is hard.

Rainwater that falls on to insoluble rock, such as slate or granite, does not have the opportunity to pick up minerals and remains more or less mineral free. This water we know as soft water.

Water hardness is subdivided into two classes: temporary hardness and permanent hardness. There are two major minerals that are mostly responsible for causing hardness in water: calcium bicarbonate (derived from chalk) and calcium sulphate (gypsum). Calcium bicarbonate hardness is known as temporary hardness because upon boiling the calcium bicarbonate is broken down into calcium carbonate (common chalk), water and carbon dioxide gas. The chalk is insoluble in water so it settles out, causing the familiar fur in kettles and pipes. However, hardness caused by calcium sulphate (gypsum) cannot be removed by boiling and this is known as permanent hardness. Most waters have both permanent and temporary hardness, but in varying degrees depending on the location of the source.

There are many minerals that can be detected in most water supplies, but only a few are important as far as brewing is concerned:

Calcium Bicarbonate Ca (HCO₃)₂

This is sometimes called calcium hydrogen carbonate, and is the principal substance causing alkalinity and temporary hardness in our water supplies. Calcium bicarbonate is derived from calcium carbonate (common chalk). Calcium carbonate is insoluble in water, but in regions where there is chalk in the substrata, the carbon dioxide gas absorbed in the rainwater during its earthward journey reacts with the carbonates, producing calcium bicarbonate, which goes into solution easily.

The type of hardness caused by bicarbonates is known as temporary hardness because it can be removed by boiling the water. During boiling the calcium bicarbonate is broken down into calcium carbonate (common chalk), water and carbon dioxide gas. The gas is given off to the atmosphere and the insoluble chalk settles out on the bottom of the vessel.

Bicarbonate is undesirable in beer and is detrimental to a number of processes. It reacts adversely with components in the mash, increasing mash pH, and it reduces mash efficiency. Bicarbonate ions interfere with the fermentation process, buffer and reduce the effect of the more important calcium ions, and mess up charge-based fining systems. Bicarbonate is also said to extract a degree of harshness from the hops.

Within this chapter the terms carbonate and bicarbonate are used somewhat interchangeably; they are similar, but they are not quite the same thing. For now, it is probably sufficient to regard calcium bicarbonate as the water-soluble form of calcium carbonate (chalk). Calcium carbonate does not dissolve much in water, so from our point of view it exists in its bicarbonate form in water.

Calcium Sulphate $CaSO_4$ (gypsum)

This is the principal substance causing hardness in the deep well waters of Burton-upon-Trent and many other areas. Calcium sulphate hardness is termed permanent hardness because the mineral cannot be removed from water by boiling. Fortunately it is a beneficial mineral as far as brewing goes. Calcium is required by a number of brewing reactions and the sulphate form is a convenient way of holding it in the water.

Sulphate is said to suppress harshness and astringent flavours. This allows a high level of hops to be used to provide a full flavour and aroma without extracting an undesirable harshness from other components of the hop. However, too much calcium sulphate is said to impart a harsh taste, particularly in the presence of high chloride levels, and runs the risk of precipitating polypeptides, hop resins and too much phosphate out of solution.

Calcium Chloride $CaCl_2$

This can be used as an alternative to the sulphate salt to provide important calcium ions without the softening or mellowing effect on flavour that the sulphate salt imparts. It can also be used as a substitute for calcium sulphate to lower mash pH. Chloride is said to promote a fullness of flavour, but it can also enhance any harshness that may exist. Chlorides can be tasted directly if used in excess. Some say that chloride levels in excess of 200 mg/litre may be required for Milds, Porters and strong dark beers. Remember that common table salt is also a chloride and will contribute to the flavour effect, but will not reduce pH. Calcium chloride is very hydroscopic and will absorb moisture from the atmosphere. It should be stored in an airtight container in a dry cool place.

Sodium Chloride NaCl

Many brewers say that a high proportion of sodium chloride is necessary to produce good dark beers, Porters and Stouts, but I am unable to see much scientific advantage in adding salt to water. Indeed, the presence of the sodium ion may permanently solubilise unwanted carbonates into the water, making them impossible to remove by boiling.

In general, any benefit of sodium chloride addition will be mostly along flavour-enhancement lines, as in domestic cooking. It will act as a flavour enhancer and contribute a fullness and mouth-feel to the ale. However, if a high level of hops is employed, the chloride can extract a harshness from them. Also, if sodium chloride is added in too high quantities the beer will taste salty. Levels greater than 850 mg/l can be poisonous to yeast. Sodium chloride does not lower the mash pH as calcium chloride does.

Magnesium Sulphate MgSO$_4$7H$_2$O (Epsom salts)

Epsom salts are present in some waters in fairly high amounts. Magnesium is an important mineral required by the yeast as a co-enzyme during fermentation, and magnesium sulphate provides this mineral in a permanent form that will not precipitate out of solution during the boil. It is said to have beneficial effects upon wort stabilisation during the boil. Magnesium sulphate is only required in trace quantities. Excessive magnesium is said to impart an astringent dryness to the beer.

Water treatment basics

As a generalisation, chalky water is alien to brewing processes. It can raise the pH of the mash to unacceptable levels and interfere with clarification and fining systems. Its buffering power makes it difficult to move the mash pH to the ideal of around 5.3. Thus the first operation of any water treatment when the water is chalky is to remove as much of the bicarbonate as possible – preferably reducing it to below 30 mg/l. Bicarbonates can be precipitated as carbonates by boiling or by neutralising with acid treatment. Many commercial brewers add mineral acids to their water – hydrochloric, sulphuric, or a mixture of both – to neutralise the carbonates. The most common and practical method for the home-brewer is to reduce bicarbonates by boiling the water before use.

Reducing the calcium bicarbonate in the water will lower mash pH. After the carbonate is removed, adding calcium in some other form such as calcium sulphate or calcium chloride will lower the pH of the mash even further and also supply the calcium ions necessary as co-enzymes for other reactions.

Water treatment, then, consists of two phases. The first phase is carbonate reduction, which means getting rid of the chalk, and the second phase is adding calcium in some other form to lower the mash pH to somewhere close to 5.3.

Carbonate reduction

A simple and foolproof method of reducing carbonates is to boil the water for half an hour or so. A good rolling boil is important to drive off the CO_2 generated and get it out of solution. For reasons too complicated to go into here, it also helps the reduction process if some calcium sulphate or calcium chloride is added during the boil.

One advantage of boiling is that it is impossible to overdo it, unlike acid treatment. The discussion below will stick to the boiling method because it is easier and more reliable.

Because water treatment by boiling is time consuming, it is best to treat the water the day before you brew. The total quantity of water required for brewing is rather more than the quantity of beer you are making.

Mash pH adjustment

The next phase is adding calcium, if necessary, to get the mash acidity close to pH 5.3. Adding calcium to the water or to the mash in the form of calcium sulphate or calcium chloride will lower the pH of the mash, which is usually necessary. The pH of the water and the pH of the mash are not the same thing. There is no point in measuring the pH of the water and expecting this to be reflected in the mash, because it will not. The calcium ions in the water react with other components in the mash, lowering the mash pH. It is mash pH that we are interested in.

The problem is that a trial-and-error approach is demanded. We will not know if the water is suitable for brewing until we brew with it, and by that time it is too late to do much about it. What I suggest is starting off with a basic water treatment and measuring the mash pH of the brew, keeping careful notes, then adjusting the water treatment if necessary for the next brew.

Simple water treatment

Because we are boiling the water to remove alkalinity (chalk or carbonate), the task of water treatment can be greatly simplified. All that remains is to add enough calcium in the form of sulphate or chloride to move the pH to where we expect it to be, assuming that there is not already enough calcium in your water.

So basically what we do for our preliminary water treatment is to remove any excessive carbonate by boiling then add the minimum level of calcium necessary to achieve good performance throughout the brewing process. This is widely accepted as 50 mg per litre of calcium, but I have plumped for 100 mg/l, just to make sure. 100 mg per litre will be contributed by adding 430 mg per litre of calcium sulphate (gypsum) or 370 mg per litre of calcium chloride. A very small amount of magnesium sulphate (Epsom salts) is added to provide magnesium as a co-enzyme for the yeast. Many worts are deficient in magnesium, but it is only required in trace amounts.

Approximately 100 mg per litre of calcium can be added to 23 litres of water by adding ten grams of calcium sulphate or by adding ten grams of calcium chloride or a mixture of both. If you are performing water treatment for the first time it is probably best to use just calcium sulphate.

Performing water treatment

Aerate your water before you begin the boil. Put the appropriate quantity of water into your brewing boiler, a few litres in excess of requirements to compensate for evaporation, and bring to the boil. Then add ten grams of calcium sulphate (gypsum) for every 23/25 litres and boil vigorously for 30 minutes. When the boiling period is complete switch off the heat and wait for the precipitate to settle out. When cool, rack the water off the precipitate into a storage vessel. Then

add one gram of magnesium sulphate (Epsom salts).

The magnesium sulphate is added last because it can interfere with the precipitation of carbonates.

Fine tuning

Measure the pH of the mash of your preliminary brew, and all your subsequent brews, and keep careful notes of the quantities of salts used and the volumes treated. If the pH of your mash is not where you want it to be, normally 5.3, then you need to adjust the quantity of calcium sulphate for your next brew. If the pH is too high, increase the quantity of salts; if the pH is too low, reduce them. If your pH is a long way out, say above 5.5 or below 5.1, then it is okay to adjust using quite large increments in the amount of salts – 50 per cent or more.

Soft water

If you are using very soft water with absolutely no alkalinity or chalk, there is no real need to boil it, except to dissolve the calcium sulphate. The treatment salts can just as validly be added to the mash tun, in direct proportion to the amount of mash liquor employed, with the balance added to the copper during the wort boil.

Soft water can be problematic. A certain amount of calcium needs to be added to the water to satisfy the co-enzyme requirements of the yeast – around 100 mg per litre for most beers – but adding this calcium can push the pH of the mash down far too low. This is because there is not enough residual alkalinity in the water to oppose the acidity generated by the added calcium.

With hard water, when we boil the water to remove alkalinity, it does not remove it all. A certain amount of residual alkalinity or carbonate/bicarbonate remains and provides a small buffering effect to raise mash pH. With soft water this buffering effect is missing, and in many cases we need to add some alkalinity to get the mash pH to where it ought to be. This is normally done by adding precipitated chalk to the mash. About 35 mg per litre of calcium carbonate is mixed in with the grist prior to mashing. In this case, though, the quantity to use is calculated on the volume of mash liquor, not the total volume. Simply multiply the volume of mash liquor by 35 to arrive at the amount of calcium carbonate to add. Home-brewing shops sell calcium carbonate, but they usually call it precipitated chalk.

To complicate fine tuning, while calcium sulphate or calcium chloride lower the pH of the mash, adding calcium carbonate or chalk raises it. Now we have two salts to jiggle with that act in opposite directions. With your preliminary brew, probably the best procedure is to add carbonate to the mash and also add 100 mg/l of calcium as sulphate or chloride to your water or to the mash. If the mash pH is still too low, add more carbonate next time. If pH is too high, add more sulphate. At no time during your fine tuning should you allow the added calcium to be much below the recommended 100 mg/l, otherwise you may have problems with clarity later on.

Adding calcium to the wort boil

The mash is not the only thing that requires calcium ions – many of the subsequent brewing processes require calcium too, particularly those that contribute to wort clarity and fining. Normally enough calcium will be carried across from the mash if a high level of calcium is present in the water or added as sulphate or chloride. However, sometimes the wort finds itself with a deficiency of calcium. This will usually show itself as poor yeast performance and poor clarity in the finished beer. This can be corrected by adding calcium to the wort boil. 50 mg per litre of calcium is a sufficient quantity, which can be supplied by adding five grams of calcium sulphate, calcium chloride or Brupaks DLS to the boil. There is no harm in adding five grams of calcium sulphate to the boil as a matter of routine.

Measuring mash pH

The pH of the mash should be measured fairly early into the mash because it gradually falls during its progress. However, allow time for the reactions to take place – five minutes or so. Usually when you have finished stirring the mash – 'mashed-in' in brewerspeak – enough time has elapsed.

If you are using pH papers, simply take a teaspoonful of mash fluid and place it on a white saucer and leave it for a few seconds to cool. Dunk the pH paper in the fluid and compare it against the colour scale using the white saucer as a background.

If you are using a pH meter, dunking the probe into the mash is not a good idea – the temperature is too high to expect good accuracy. You need to draw off the fluid, either using a turkey-baster or via the tap, then allow it to cool before measuring the pH.

Sodium metabisulphite and chlorine

Some home-brewers are worried that chlorine or chloramine in the water will produce a medicinal off-taste in beer. I suppose there is some substance to these fears, but in my view they are more or less groundless. There is no doubt that excessive chlorine will cause an off-taste, but this would more likely be the result of cleaning-chemical residues, rather than tap water. Chlorine in tap water is at very low levels and is very unstable and volatile, so the boil will drive any chlorine off instantly.

Despite what others may say, TCP off-tastes in beer are almost always caused by infection, not the water. Nevertheless, there is an easy way of neutralising both chlorine and chloramine in water, and that is by using sodium metabisulphite or potassium metabisulphite. Miniscule amounts are required to do the job, about five micrograms per litre, although it will not matter if it is overdone, even grossly overdone. Campden tablets are easier than trying to measure micrograms of powder. Half a campden tablet added to every 25 litres of water will do the job. If you are using a powdered metabisulphite, a generous pinch of the stuff will do it.

Water treatment for malt extract beers

Generally speaking, malt extract beers do not need water treatment because the critical mashing stage has already been performed. However, if you are brewing in a hard water area and you are experiencing clarity problems, then the high alkalinity of your water is probably affecting your beer. Water treatment can be limited to just boiling your water first and perhaps adding five grams of calcium to your wort boil as an insurance measure.

Home-brewing Equipment

Most of the equipment required to brew beer is relatively inexpensive. It can be purchased from home-brew shops, and those with practical skills and basic workshop facilities can fabricate some of it. Many home-brewers start off with kits before graduating to more advanced brewing methods. This way the basics bits and bobs – fermentation vessels, casks or bottles, hydrometers and thermometers – will already have been acquired. With the purchase of a boiler, the most expensive single item, a move to malt extract brewing can take place. At a later stage, the acquisition of a mash tun and, preferably, a hot liquor tank will allow the transition to full mash brewing.

The advantages to this staged approach is that equipment is acquired over a period of time in a financially painless manner, and basic brewing skills are gained in easily manageable stages. It can be quite daunting to launch straight into full-mash brewing without any previous experience.

If you are starting from scratch and going straight into full mash, you might consider purchasing a full-mash starter kit from one of the better home-brew shops. Kits usually include a mash tun, boiler, fermenter, thermometer and hydrometer, and sometimes a bit of run-off tubing. You will also need casks and/or bottles, a cooler, and numerous bits and bobs

such as pH papers, stirring spoons and a hydrometer trial jar.

The table opposite shows the basics required. Beer kits are included in the table to show the transition from kit to full-mash brewing. The table is arranged from preliminary stuff at the top to full-mash at the bottom. It is by no means comprehensive.

Fermenting vessels

At least one fermenting vessel is required. Traditional cask ale is fermented using a top-working yeast in an open fermenting vessel. Plastic bins are the fermenters used by the majority of British home-brewers and these

EQUIPMENT LIST

	Kits	Malt Extract	Full Mash
Fermenting vessel	Required	Required	Required
Casks	Required	Required	Required
Bottles & accessories	Optional	Optional	Optional
Thermometer	Required	Required	Required
Hydrometer & trial jar	Required	Required	Required
Volumetric measures	N/A	Required	Required
Weighing equipment	N/A	Required	Required
Boiler	N/A	Required	Required
Cooler	N/A	Desirable	Desirable
Mash tun	N/A	N/A	Required
Hot liquor tank	N/A	N/A	Desirable
pH measurement	N/A	N/A	Desirable

closely imitate the open fermenters of the traditional British commercial brewery. These bins come with a lid that can be fitted if it is thought necessary to protect the beer, although some yeasts do not perform as well when totally enclosed, so protection is usually only required at the beginning and end of fermentation, if at all.

More than one bin is a good idea. Five-gallon brewing bins are useful general-purpose things to have around the brewery. The standard fermentation bin has a number of additional uses, such as holding sparge liquor, collecting spargings, lugging water into the garage/ brewery, mashing, cleaning and disinfecting bits and bobs.

The bins come in two varieties: the traditional tapered, bucket-shaped type and the more cylindrical bin. The cylindrical bins are narrower, taller and straighter than the buckets and I prefer them because the wort is a bit deeper and the top surface area smaller,

exposing less to the atmosphere and making it easier for yeast-head formation and skimming. Both types come with close-fitting lids and are available with or without taps.

For bottom-working yeasts, lagers, or when you feel an enclosed fermenter is more appropriate, a standard home-brew cask may be used as a fermenter. A cheaper option is the enclosed fermenting vessel available from home-brewing shops with a four-inch cap, probably intended for winemaking but equally suitable as a brewing fermenter.

One aspect of these bins that is worth mentioning is calibration. The bins usually have graduations printed on the side that are supposed to indicate the volume of the liquid inside, but these are notoriously inaccurate. It is useful to have some method of measuring large volumes of fluid to a reasonable degree of accuracy – the answer is to calibrate your bins yourself.

By the time you get to the end of this chapter you will have decided to get yourself a set of electronic household scales if you do not already have some lurking in your kitchen. To calibrate your bin, take a plastic kitchen jug, place it on your scales, and set the weight to zero. Carefully add water to the jug until the weight is exactly one kilogram. To save repeating this 25 or 30 times, make a mark on the jug at the water line with tape or an indelible pen. You then have a fairly accurate, repeatable measurement for one litre of water.

Repeatedly fill the jug to the datum line (the mark) and add the contents to your fermenter, marking off the levels on the fermenter with the indelible pen as you go. You can usually get away with five-litre graduations up to about 15 or 20 litres and one-litre graduations after that until you reach the brim of the bin. Then you have a calibrated bin.

Alternatively, the method I prefer is to use a 600 mm (two-foot) stainless-steel rule to measure the depth of the water at each stage, keeping the rule perfectly vertical and perpendicular to the bottom. I make a note of volume against depth and at a later stage I plot this on a graph on the computer – a straight line through all the points. You can then easily interpolate to any volume you wish. In my case I calculated the volume against depth mathematically by accurately measuring the internal dimensions of the bin and applying them to a formula.

Once you have your calibration chart, there is no need to dip the rule into the beer to take a measurement. Your chart can also show the volume depending on the amount of empty space from the rim of the bin to the surface of the beer, or you can gauge from the outside. A torch shone inside the vessel is a good way of showing up the level on thick plastic when gauging from the outside.

Casks

When you have brewed your beer you will obviously need some form of container in which to mature and keep it, and to dispense it from. Even if you are bottling your beer, it is desirable to give it some time conditioning in the cask first, so at least one cask is a necessity. Casks come in two price ranges. The cheaper budget casks are adequate, but there are benefits to obtaining the more robust and correspondingly expensive premium casks – they have a large four-inch neck and cap, big enough to get a hand in, and a tap with a proper back-nut. Indeed, because a back-nut can be fitted, the cask can be retro-fitted with any tap of choice.

Premium casks come in two varieties, with either a top tap or a bottom tap. The bottom tap is the one to go for. The top-tap types are an abomination in my view – the beer cannot be dispensed naturally, by gravity, but must be dispensed by top pressure. If you run out of gas you are stuck. The top taps have a floating take-off system that draws the beer from the surface. Not only does this encourage the drinking of green beer, before it has cleared down properly and matured, but the top layer is usually the oxidised layer, so slow drinkers are always drinking oxidised beer. The top layer contains any floaters – bits of hop from dry hopping for example. These usually end up blocking the float or the tap. The float is just a push fit into the tap and often becomes disconnected and, finally, the float has a habit of turning itself upside down, making the drawing off of beer impossible.

Most casks have caps fitted with a CO_2 injector valve as standard. It is a good idea to get a spare set of all the washers and seals; a stock of tap-sealing washers is handy as well as a couple of O-rings that seal the cap. The rubbers for the gas injector and pressure-relief valve need replacing from time to time, so it is also useful to have spares of those.

When cleaning and disinfecting the cask, make sure that the internals of the tap are also cleaned and disinfected. From time to time remove the tap, dismantle it, and give it a thorough clean out. Separate the O-ring from the cap to ensure that both cap and ring are properly disinfected and nothing nasty is lurking under the seal. Give the O-ring a light smear of petroleum jelly (Vaseline) before refitting it to help ensure a perfect seal. The threads of the caps should also be given a smear of petroleum jelly to make them run smoothly. A useful accessory is a cap spanner to help remove difficult caps. These are available from home-brewing suppliers. The tap-sealing washer, by the way, should be fitted to the outside of the cask, not the inside.

Unfortunately, most of the casks available to home-brewers are too big. Ideally the cask should be quite full when the ale is stowed away for maturation. Air is the enemy of sound beer. The best way of keeping air out of contact with the beer is to make sure there is no room for it.

Home-brew casks vary in size and the internal volume is often much larger than the quoted nominal volume. With a standard brew of five gallons, there is often a good deal of empty space (ullage) that is initially full of air, and beer condition is wasted pressurising the empty space. The effects of this can be minimised by purging out most of the air by carefully venting – a couple of days after filling, undo the cap to release the pressure, then close the cap tightly again. I usually perform this operation twice, a few days apart. Because CO_2 is heavier than air, the air sits on top and is expelled first, as long as the cask has been left undisturbed for a while beforehand. You'll never get all the air out because it does mix with CO_2 to a small degree. A full cask is a better bet.

Bottles and bottling accessories

Although many brewers dispense their beer from cask, bottles may be more convenient for those who do not drink at a sufficiently fast rate to dispose of five gallons before the beer goes off. Well-brewed bottled beer will keep for many months, even years, without deterioration, and most styles will improve with age. The advantage of bottled beer is that you are not restricted to drinking just the beer from the one cask that has been recently broached. Instead, in time, the brewer will have a stock of several different types of beer, of different ages, to choose from; an enviable well-stocked cellar. The major disadvantage of bottled beer is the chore of cleaning and disinfecting 40 one-pint bottles or 46 500 ml bottles and then filling them. It is this that puts many brewers off bottling.

Suitable glass bottles are available from home-brew shops, but there are other sources of used bottles that are a cheaper option. They must be capable of withstanding pressure, and preferably brown. Brown bottles are better because beer is sensitive to ultraviolet light and exposure to sunlight or bright fluorescent lights can cause chemical changes to occur within the beer. Brown bottles filter this light out. Used beer bottles are obviously a good bet. It is fine to use disposable bottles and lightweight bottles as long as they are meant for pressurised, carbonated drinks.

Accessories you will need for bottling include bottle tops, known as crown caps, and a capping tool, both available from home-brew shops. There are three types of capping tool: the hammer-on type (don't ask, give that one a miss), a two-handled capper, and a one-handled bench capper that looks like a drill press. The two-handled capper is the most popular type, easy to use and adequate. The bench capper looks more professional and is probably easier, but more expensive. If you intend to collect any particular type of ex-beer bottle in quantity, try capping one first. Apparently some micro-breweries use a bottle that is difficult to cap with the modern two-handled capper. Don't forget to sterilise your caps before bottling.

A bottle brush for cleaning is essential. Always rinse bottles immediately after use to avoid any dried-on deposits and to make life easier later. A syphon – a length of flexible tube with a rigid pipe fitted at one end that reaches right to the bottom of the bottle – will be required for bottle filling. The long rigid pipe is necessary to prevent air getting into the beer (which will reduce its shelf life) and to minimise foaming. You can buy a bottling stick which is a rigid pipe with an automatic valve fitted at the bottom which makes filling much easier and reduces beer wastage.

Plastic PET (polyethylene terephthalate) bottles have a number of uses within the home brewery: for making yeast starters, for keeping hydrometers and thermometers in a weak disinfectant during a brewing session and, perhaps, for transporting manageable quantities of beer to a venue. They are not good, however, for storage of beer – in fact they are very bad at it.

The problem is that PET bottles leak. No, they do not leak fluids, they leak gas – like a sieve. Oxygen diffuses through the plastic from the outside in, and carbon dioxide diffuses from the inside out. They leak so badly that a carbonated drink can lose 15 per cent of its carbonation in just four weeks. The diffusion of oxygen into the bottle can oxidise a susceptible product just as quickly, causing staling. More importantly, PET bottles, by their very nature, are one-trip, single-use only. Even junk beer is rarely packaged in PET and quality beer is never packaged in PET.

Thermometer

A good quality thermometer is an essential item. Glass spirit thermometers available from home-brewing shops are adequate. It is advantageous to stick with 30 cm semi-precision thermometers and not mess around with smaller ones or floating thermometers and the like. Glass thermometers are only fully accurate at their calibrated immersion depth. This is usually indicated with a mark or a line on the stem somewhere below the scale, or with the immersion depth printed in figures on the back –

it is usually 76 mm. Deviations from the immersion depth will result in deviations from the true temperature reading. If there is no line, assume that it is either not a quality thermometer or it is a full-immersion thermometer (which is inappropriate for home-brewing). Glass thermometers have a habit of rolling off work tops, so more than one is a good idea. Even if you are going electronic, at least one glass thermometer as an emergency standby is useful.

Electronic thermometers are the thing these days and it will not be long before glass thermometers are relegated to museums and the *Antiques Roadshow*. However, bear in mind that the really cheap electronic types are of dubious accuracy and often do not last five minutes in the home-brewing environment.

Hydrometer

A hydrometer is a useful and inexpensive item of equipment that enables us to measure the specific gravity of our wort at various stages during fermentation. It tells us how much sugar is in the wort at the start of fermentation and how much is left during the course of fermentation. The typical brewer's open glass hydrometer used with a trial jar is most suitable for our purposes.

The density of a fluid is temperature dependent and hydrometers are calibrated for use at a particular temperature, usually 20°C in the case of most brewing hydrometers, but 15.6°C (60°F) is common too. With good quality hydrometers the measurement temperature is printed on the stem somewhere. To correct for temperature, a correction factor is added or subtracted from the indicated gravity reading. Hot fluids should be cooled as close as possible to the calibration temperature before measurement is attempted because greater errors occur at higher temperatures. Temperature correction tables for 20°C and 15.6°C hydrometers are provided on *p199*.

The hydrometers available to home-brewers are sometimes rather cheap and cheerful, woefully inadequate and meet no standards in particular. Some home-brewing shops do supply better quality hydrometers such as the Stevenson Reeves S1500 Easy Hydrometer, which is good for beer because it is not cluttered with superfluous scales and is easy to read. All we brewers need to know is specific gravity – accurately.

General-purpose 250 mm laboratory hydrometers are preferred by many home-brewers and are superior to most of the examples supplied through the home-brewing trade. They are reasonably priced (about three or four pints of pub beer) and are made to BS specs with a guaranteed accuracy. There are two types of general-purpose hydrometer: specific gravity and density. For our purposes, either is fine. As long as the density hydrometer is scaled in units of g/ml (or g/cm3), which is usual, the numbers tie up and are equivalent so we can use either type. Note that general-purpose specific gravity hydrometers are calibrated for 15.6°C (60°F) and density hydrometers for 20°C. This again makes no difference as long as we are aware of it. A specific gravity range of 1000 to 1100 is adequate for almost all beers, and the scale of a 250 mm hydrometer is relatively easy to read.

Using the hydrometer

A hydrometer should never be held out horizontally by the stem – it will break. Hold it vertically above the scale, as finger grease lower down can affect its accuracy.

1 *Before taking a measurement, make sure the hydrometer, trial jar and thermometer are perfectly clean – accuracy will be affected by dirt on the hydrometer. Also make sure they are disinfected if you intend to pour the sample back into your beer.*

2 *Fill your trial jar. If the temperature of the sample is much higher than the temperature printed on the hydrometer, allow it to cool naturally or force cool it by standing the jar in some cold water. Give the sample a stir from time to time to equalise the temperature.*

3 *Carefully insert the hydrometer into the wort or beer, holding it at the top of the stem, and release it gently when it is approximately at its position of equilibrium.*

4 *Give the hydrometer a gentle spin to release CO_2 bubbles clinging to it which can raise the hydrometer higher in the beer and give a higher than true reading. Stop the spin by gripping the top of the stem, then give the stem a very small downward depression into the beer and wait for the bouncing to stabilise. Ensure that the hydrometer is not touching the side of the trial jar.*

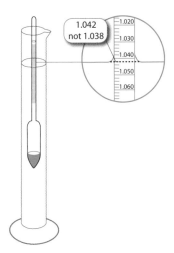

1.042 not 1.038

-1.020
-1.030
-1.040
-1.050
-1.060

5 *Take the reading at eye level through the liquid. The correct reading is at the bottom of the meniscus on the same plane as the surface of the beer, not at the top of the meniscus where the surface of the liquid actually touches the hydrometer. Take the reading before more CO_2 bubbles cling to the sides again.*

6 *Take a temperature reading immediately afterwards and, if necessary, correct the reading for*

temperature by using the temperature-correction tables (see p199). If the temperature is much different from ambient, it is better to take two temperature measurements, one immediately before and one immediately after taking the SG measurement, then find the average.

Like thermometers, hydrometers have a habit of rolling off work tops and breaking, leaving the brewer stranded. It is a good idea to have more than one.

Weight and volume measurement

The measurement of small quantities is often required in home-brewing: cleaning chemicals, water treatment salts, Irish moss, finings, etc. Kitchen spoons and cups are okay for most things, but sometimes something a little less hit and miss is required. Plastic or stainless-steel measuring cups are a useful accessory. They usually come as a set of four or six with a range of sizes from about 25 ml up to 250 ml. Do not, however, rely on the calibrations on kitchen measuring jugs. Accurate measurement of small volumes of liquid can be achieved by calibrated medicine syringes available from pharmacies. These are available in a range of sizes from 5 ml up to about 25 ml.

It is almost a prerequisite for home-brewers to own a set of digital kitchen scales. These are the only easily-available gadgets that can be used to weigh, say, 25 grams of hops with reasonable accuracy.

Boiler

A boiler (called a 'copper' in brewerspeak) capable of boiling a full batch of beer is an essential item of equipment whether you are making full-mash or malt extract beers. We need to boil large volumes of wort, sometimes in excess of our final volume of beer, if we sparge over-enthusiastically.

There are several types of boiler available to us. The home-brew industry supplies a range of electric boilers of various sorts, and there are commercial types intended for the catering industry which can be adapted for home-brewing.

The boilers made specifically for home-brewing are usually based on plastic bins or buckets with a kettle element fitted as a heater. However, these days kettle elements are harder to find, because most modern kettles have integral, concealed, non-replaceable elements. Also, people do not bother to repair kettles any more. Thus the supply of spare elements is diminishing and likely to dry up completely sometime in the near future. A likely substitute is the 11-inch, 3kW immersion heater element, at least until something better surfaces. Although there are issues with fitting immersion heater elements, they are better than kettle elements for various, slightly technical, reasons.

There are a couple of well-known brands of the plastic bin type of boiler, that are supplied by the wholesalers to the shops, but some shops construct their own. The shop-built ones are often better value and have a hop strainer fitted. Some have twin elements that allow the contents to reach the boil faster, after which one of the elements can be switched off for the duration of the boil.

It doesn't hurt to have a boiler somewhat larger than the brew volume (known as brew length). There will be a certain amount of foam generated part way through the boil, and although this foam can be controlled and minimised if you happen to be watching it, rather like boiling milk it always foams suddenly the minute your back is turned. Additional headroom reduces the risk of a messy boil-over. Once this foaming phase has passed, the boil can be left to get on with it. Sometimes we oversparge and end up with more wort than our brew length. A larger boiler will accommodate this.

My own boiler is only 26 litres capacity, plus a small amount of headroom, and I cope with it well enough, but a slightly larger boiler would be better. My brewing procedure is tailored so that I try not end up with more wort than the brew length. If I do have a bit more wort than the boiler can cope with, I keep it in a jug and add it to the boil as the volume reduces due to evaporation. My boiler is an old 26-litre Burco; the modern Burcos are 30 litres. This should be more than adequate for a five-gallon brew length.

A complication with home-brewing boilers is that because we boil the hops in the wort, we need a method of filtering or straining out the hops during run-off to separate them from the wort and preventing them blocking the tap. A hop bag is one solution to this problem but it is better to boil the hops freely in the wort and use a hop strainer fitted within the boiler. When buying a boiler for home-brewing, ensure it is fitted with a hop strainer. If you are adapting a catering boiler, you will need to fit your own hop strainer or use a hop bag.

Hop back (hop bag, hop strainer)

As well as a copper, commercial brewers use a separate vessel called a hop back to separate the hops from the wort after the boil. Their taps and associated pipework are large enough to allow the hops to pass through from the copper to hop back, but ours usually are not, so rather than use two vessels to perform this function we have a combined copper and hop back. Our hop back is a strainer of some sort that fits into the boiler.

The simplest of all hop strainers is a coarse-mesh, open bag suspended in the boiler. The home-brewing industry supplies coarse-mesh muslin hop bags for this purpose. One objection to these bags is that they can restrict the all-important vigour of the boil. Ideally the hops should be allowed to boil freely in the wort. Furthermore,

during the run off the hops perform a secondary function of forming a filter bed that filters out the trub produced during the boil; hop bags can impede this function. Nevertheless, many brewers use them to their complete satisfaction.

The more usual type of strainer is a copper-tube matrix, which is an arrangement of slotted pipes that sits flat against the bottom of the boiler and is connected to the outlet tap by a small length of flexible tubing. These are available from home-brew shops, but many home-brewers make their own from standard copper plumbing tubing, 90° bends and T-pieces. For ease of fabrication 22 mm pipe is usually used, but 15 mm is as good and gives a little less dead space.

Four lengths of tube (actually three plus two half-lengths) are assembled into a square-shaped matrix, using four 90° bends with a T-piece in the two half-lengths for the take-off pipe. If 22 mm tube is used the T-piece will probably need to be a 22 mm x 22 mm to 15 mm reducer-T to fit the take-off pipe. Usually an additional crosspiece (sometimes several) is added that bisects the square to increase the active area, necessitating another length of tube and two equal Ts. A number of slots are cut with a hacksaw across each of the exposed lengths of tube about a third of the way through the pipe, at intervals of about 10 mm. The slots face downwards against the base of the boiler when the contraption is fitted. It is not essential to solder the matrix together – they can be a push-fit – although soldering will reduce the dead space a bit.

Thermostats, simmerstats

Many boilers are fitted with a regulator of some sort – either a thermostat or a simmerstat. A thermostat measures temperature and turns the heater on and off as appropriate. A simmerstat is an energy controller that regulates the power into the heater by switching the heater on for a variable period depending on setting, and then off for the remainder of the switching cycle.

Both devices can be more trouble than they are worth when it comes to wort boiling. Simmerstats may not turn up to full power and will annoyingly keep switching off every 30 seconds or so, taking the wort off the boil.

CAUTION

Attempting to move 25 litres of hot wort or hot water from one position to another can result in an unscheduled visit to A&E. Tailor your brewing process so that there is never any need to move large volumes of hot sticky fluids. Ensure that the platform on which vessels such as your boiler stand is stable and out of reach of inquisitive children and animals. Wear sensible footwear – it is often the feet that cop the worst of it. Do not rely on the handles of bins to support the weight of 25 litres of hot fluid.

Thermostats fitted to catering boilers seem to top out at 93°C, perhaps to prevent people accidentally boiling the contents away, but probably because of some EEC directive. In this case the wort never reaches the boil, which is not what we need.

It is often necessary to doctor these things, sometimes by dismantling them and modifying them internally by those who are competent in such things, but more often by bypassing them, either permanently or with a bypass switch. It is not necessary to have a regulator for wort boiling; full thrutch is all that is required. However, if you are going to use a boiler as a hot liquor tank, some form of control is useful, although not essential.

If you are buying a boiler with a regulator fitted, get assurances from the supplier that the boiler will boil continuously and uninterrupted. Fitting a by-pass switch is not rocket science but requires some competence in the art of electrickery. With twin-element boilers, a regulator fitted to one element and not to the other gives the best of both worlds.

Cooler

A useful but optional extra is a cooling system to bring the temperature of the wort down to pitching temperature after the boil. For generations home-brewers have simply run the wort from the boiler into a disinfected bin, fitted a disinfected close-fitting lid, and left it overnight to cool. Standing the bin in a bath of cold water speeds up cooling, but it can still take hours, even with constant agitation.

A more modern approach is to use an immersion cooler. This is a coil of copper tube placed into the boiler at the end of the boil, through which cold water from the tap is run. These are available from home-brewing shops, but it is relatively easy to make your own with ten metres of 10 mm soft copper microbore tube, which can be purchased from any DIY emporium. Wrap it around a suitable former, a demijohn for example, into a close coil. The diameter of the coil should be smaller than the internal diameter of the boiler so that there is plenty of room for wort circulation around the full surface area of the coil. Technically, cooling water should enter the bottom of the coil and exit at the top, but many home-brewers say that the wort cools more quickly if it is operated the wrong way round. The wort will be cooled to pitching temperature (below 25°C) in 20-40 minutes depending on conditions. I will leave it to your own ingenuity to work out how to fit hoses to each end.

My own cooler is a coil of tubing permanently plumbed inside a standard wide-neck home-brewing cask. When the cap is fitted I can safely move the cask elsewhere, should I wish. The handles on most casks can safely take the weight of 25 litres, whereas those on most brewing bins cannot, and the thick plastic does not go soft and squidgy when hot. It does, however, take me twice as long as everybody else to cool my wort,

but then I do not seem to be in such a hurry as everybody else. And it is yet another vessel to clean.

Mashing equipment

Mashing is the process of infusing crushed malted barley grain in water at a carefully maintained temperature of about 66°C, which enables the enzymes to convert the starch in the malt into fermentable sugars. Commercial breweries mash using a vessel called a mash tun. This is an unheated, well-insulated vessel with a perforated false bottom to retain the grain so that the wort can easily be drained from the mash. The vessel relies on good thermal insulation to maintain the temperature.

The mash tun is a simple vessel in principle, but it is the most awkward item in our home-brewing armoury and fairly complicated in some respects. It has three critical functions to perform. It must hold the temperature of a batch of grain and liquor at a constant temperature of around 66°C for a period of 90 minutes to two hours without the temperature falling appreciably. It must have a filter that holds back the crushed grain and allows the sweet wort to run off, separating the wort from the grain without the grain bed blocking the filter. Finally comes sparging – the rinsing of the grains with a very fine shower of hot liquor to flush out all the sugars. The sparge should be extremely slow and gentle – the sparge liquor should be evenly distributed over the surface of the mash and the flow rate of sparge liquor input and run-off output should be balanced such that bits and pieces in the mash tun remain floating and do not compact down onto the filter and block it.

Many home-brewing mash tuns meet some of the above criteria, but few meet them all. The temperature maintenance is performed by good thermal insulation around the sides and top of the tun; old blankets or quilts have been pressed into service for this, but better still is tank insulation or thick foam camping mats. The grain filter can be a tube matrix as described for the wort boiler previously, but better still is a false bottom. Sparging is a difficult one because it must be a slow and gentle process and achieved with just a short head of water.

Buying a mash tun

Some of the better home-brewing shops supply ready-made mash tuns. These are based on standard, rectangular, picnic-style cool boxes fitted with a tap and a slotted tube matrix to serve as the mash filter. Some are fitted with sparging apparatus but most are not.

Beware of the type of boiler sold by most home-brewing shops that is advertised as a 'mashing bin'. It isn't – it is just a bucket with a 2.4kW kettle element in it. There is, of course, no reason why it cannot be used as a passive mash tun by fitting a grain bag or a mash filter and some

insulation, but do not rely on the heater to maintain the temperature – it is too risky. The fact that the contents of the mash tun is a bad conductor of heat, the slow response time and poor sensitivity of the thermostat, the relatively high wattage of the element, and the high energy-density of the physically small kettle element fitted (a lot of energy pumped into a small space), can all conspire to cause the surface of the element to exceed a safe temperature – anything up to or above 100°C. This will at best denature the enzymes, causing poor mash efficiency, and at worst produce a thick glutenous mash; a porridge-like gloop that will cause a set mash.

It is a boiler and that is what it should be used for. To use it as a mash tun, the heater can be used to raise the liquor to strike temperature before the grain is added, but be wary of using the element when the mash is in progress. The bin should be insulated to maintain temperature.

Home-made insulated mash tun

You will need a well-insulated bin with a tap fitted to enable run-off to be performed. The easiest way of putting together a mash tun is to add a grain bag to the bin, available from home-brewing shops. A grain bag is simply a large, nylon, fine-mesh bag that fits inside the brewing bin and holds back the grain during run-off and sparging. The bag is held in place by clipping it to the sides of the bin with bulldog clips or clothes pegs. When using a grain bag, it is a good idea to put something like a dinner plate on the bottom of the bin, resting on the top of the tap outlet, to prevent the bag and grain from 'smothering' the outlet and blocking it. When purchasing your grain bag, try it in a bin of the same size to ensure that it fits snugly against the sides of the bin. If it doesn't, you will not be able to sparge efficiently because the liquor will run down the sides rather than percolate through the grains.

Alternatively, you can fabricate a mash tun from a picnic cool box, similar to the ones supplied by home-brewing shops. A slotted-tube matrix can be used as a mash filter, just as in the shop-supplied ones. Bear in mind that with some of the cheaper cool boxes insulation is not particularly efficient – home-brewers often dismantle the box, remove the polystyrene insulation blocks and re-insulate with polyurethane foam, as well as adding external insulation. Very often the lids of these things have no insulation at all, and it is through the top that most of the heat is lost.

Another home-made mash tun

My favourite style of mash tun is simply a standard brewing bin fitted with a perforated false bottom. I prefer the false bottom approach because, in theory at least, it gives a more distributed run-off than a typical tube-matrix, reducing the likelihood of the wort channelling through the

goods as a rivulet rather than percolating evenly and rinsing out the sugars as it should. A round mash tun lends itself better to a rotating sparge arm than a rectangular box.

Perforated false bottoms can be purchased, but they appear and disappear from the home-brew trade with monotonous regularity, and they are expensive. It is a straightforward matter to fabricate a false bottom from a plastic, melamine, picnic or barbecue plate – an idea I picked up from a chap who signs himself Daab on an Internet home-brewing forum. Ten-inch melamine plates seem to be the largest commonly available and they fit nicely into the bottom of a fermenting bin.

Depending on the design of the mash tun, the centre of the plate may or may not be drilled to take an adapter for fitting a take-off pipe. The remainder of the plate is drilled with a large number of evenly-spaced 2 mm holes – the more the better – to act as the strainer.

Insulating the mash tun

The mash tun must be very well insulated during the mashing period, otherwise the temperature will drop too much. All sorts of methods have been used for insulation – old blankets and quilts being common. For years I used plastic-covered water-tank insulation wrapped around the bin and held in place by luggage straps. During the mash more strips of insulation are laid over the top to reduce heat loss through the lid.

A more elegant approach is to use thick foam camping mats. These are waterproof and insulate well. They too can be affixed by luggage straps, or they can be cut to size and permanently fixed to the bin with duct tape or a strong adhesive. Camping mats are available in a variety of thicknesses up to about 1.2 cm. The thicker the better – two or three layers are normally required.

Most heat loss is through the top of the bin, so pay special attention to insulating the lid. You can also place a circle of camping mat or bubble wrap on the surface of the mash before fitting the lid. Removing the lid to measure temperature or pH will result in significant heat loss, so this should be kept to a minimum. Once the mash is in progress it is best left to its own devices.

Sparging equipment

Sparging entails spraying hot water at a temperature of around 80°C over the contents of the mash tun to rinse out the sugars. It is a slow, gentle operation. Many home-brewers attempt to sparge too quickly. The trick to thorough sparging, apart from patience, is not to drain the mash bed completely, but to keep it floating. This requires careful balancing of the inflow and outflow of the tun, such that the sugars are gradually flushed by a process of continual dilution. You need something that will produce enough of a fine and gentle spray to do the job at the necessary slow pace without breaking up the grain bed and causing channelling.

Commercial brewers sparge with a rotating sparge arm. Home-brewing versions of these are available, but they can be hard to find and expensive.

A crude way of sparging is to gently pour jugs of hot water over the surface of the mash, but this can have the disadvantage of breaking up the mash bed too much. To avoid this you can put a layer of aluminium kitchen foil on the surface of the mash, perforated with a multitude of small holes, to disperse the water and break its force. This is probably the most popular method because it is the easiest, and does not require a boiler or hot liquor tank to command the mash tun.

Another method is to use a small watering can to spray hot water over the surface of the mash or, better still, a watering can rose connected to a boiler or hot liquor tank via a length of tubing. A small, fine rose intended for indoor plants or seedlings is most appropriate.

A simple and effective method of sparging is to lay a length of small-bore flexible plastic tubing, 8 mm bore or less, on the surface of the mash. The tubing is connected to your boiler or hot liquor tank in some manner, usually by stepping down from larger-size tubing that will fit the tap. The outlet end lies on, or just below, the surface of the fluid in the mash. The last few inches of the tubing are formed into a bit of a spiral so that the sparge liquor issuing from the outlet creates a gentle circular whirlpool motion. Keep the mash bed floating by balancing the outflow to the inflow.

In the absence of sparging equipment, the instructions for grain brewing on *p75* give a simple method of rinsing the sugars from the grains using a re-mashing technique that commercial brewers used before sparge arms were invented. It is less efficient than proper sparging, though.

Hot liquor tank

A hot liquor tank is useful but not essential. It maintains the sparge liquor at an appropriate temperature during sparging. If you don't have one the main wort boiler can be used for this operation and the sweet wort collected in an intermediate vessel then transferred to the boiler when sparging is over.

A second boiler is often pressed into service as a hot liquor tank. Or one can be fabricated from an enclosed wide-necked fermenter, sometimes fitted with an immersion heater, but nevertheless well insulated with camping mat material. In this case a thermostat or simmerstat is useful to maintain the temperature.

pH measurement

Measurement of pH is an essential requirement for mashers, primarily to check that the acidity of the mash is within range. As well as the mash, the remainder of the brewing process, particularly fining processes, are also pH sensitive. If the pH of the mash is correct and sufficient calcium is present in your wort, the pH of subsequent processes should fall into place automatically. The mash should be within the range of pH 5.1 to pH 5.6 with pH 5.3 being optimum.

pH papers are by far the most convenient method of measuring and are inexpensive and easy to use. pH papers cover specific ranges of pH values. Papers that cover pH 5.2 to pH 6.7 will be the most useful, but an additional set covering lower values, say pH 3.8 to pH 5.5, will almost certainly come in handy.

A few minutes into the mash, simply take a drop of fluid and place it on a white saucer – leave it a few seconds to cool then dip the paper into it. Compare the resulting colour against the white background of the saucer to the colour scale supplied with the papers.

Electronic pH meters are also available, but good ones are expensive, and cheap ones are of dubious accuracy. Most home-brewers regard pH meters as a pain because they need to be calibrated against standard buffer solutions each time you use them; the probe/ electrode is a consumable and has a shelf life of just six months whether you use it or not; and the gums in the mash tend to block the porous surface of the electrode. Many home-brewers, after experimenting with a meter, revert to pH papers.

For practical purposes it is immaterial whether mash pH is measured at room temperature or mash temperature. Common sense would dictate that mash pH is always measured at room temperature; indeed, when using pH papers (which are standardised at 25°C) there is no detectable difference anyway. Mash pH does not shift much with temperature and, even when using a pH meter, the reading at room temperature would, at most, be 0.1pH higher than at mash temperature, so pH5.2 to pH5.7 at room temperature would be equivalent to pH5.1 to pH5.6 at mash temperature, but the difference is not worth worrying about.

Siphoning

If we British are renowned for our inventive genius, our scientific acumen and our brilliant application to all things technical, why is it that our siphon tubes float? The home-brewing industry has been established for many years but it still supplies us with siphon tubes that float or get dragged out of the wort by their own weight. The glass siphon attachments break as soon as you look at them and the plastic attachments fall apart at critical moments. A task that should be the simplest of all home-brew operations – siphoning a fluid from one vessel to another – often turns out to be the most difficult.

The solution to this problem is to obtain a couple of 11 inch (280 mm) lengths of stainless steel motor vehicle brake piping or small-bore copper tubing and insert these into the ends of the siphon tube. The pipe should be very slightly larger than the inside diameter of the siphon tubing. The plastic siphon tubing is softened by dunking it in hot water, and it is then forced onto the end of the brake pipe. Hey presto! You have a siphon tube that stays under the surface of the beer. These extensions also make bottle filling a two-handed rather than three-handed operation and reduce the possibility of excessive aeration. It is easy to thrust the pipe to the bottom of the bottle while controlling the flow by squeezing the siphon tubing. Aeration is eliminated and sound beer is assured.

A large old-fashioned bulldog clip will clamp siphon tubing to the edge of your fermentation bin and save it from being dragged out of the bin by its own weight. Pet shops sell widgets, intended for fish-tank aerators, that will clamp onto your siphon tubing and enable you to adjust the flow should you wish to do so.

A really good gadget to have for bottling is a bottle filling stick. This is a length of rigid tubing with a stop-valve on the end. When you remove it from the bottle the flow automatically cuts off. It makes bottling a much less messy operation.

Cleaning and Disinfecting

There is a lot of cleaning involved in this hobby and it is not something that can be neglected or skimped because, sooner or later, it will catch you out. One of the keystones to making consistently good and stable beer is to pay proper attention to cleanliness and disinfection.

Wort and beer are perfect culture mediums, full of nutrients and trace elements, ideal for the growth of moulds, bacteria, wild yeast and numerous other nasties that will infect your beer.

Needless to say, everything that comes into contact with wort or beer should be thoroughly cleaned immediately after use and disinfected before the next use. This includes not only your bins, casks and bottles, but your hydrometers and thermometers, trial jars, measuring vessels and even bottle tops.

Cleaning and disinfecting are usually two separate operations. Most cleaners do not disinfect particularly well and most disinfectants do not clean particularly well. The two operations are also performed at different times – cleaning immediately after equipment is used and disinfecting immediately before equipment is used.

Cleaning

Cleaning means removing dirt and organic matter that can harbour bacteria and supply nutrients for those bacteria. Fortunately, the majority of home-brewing equipment is made from smooth-sided, non-porous materials such as plastic, stainless-steel or glass which are easy to clean if tackled promptly. If these items are rinsed and cleaned immediately after use, before deposits have dried on, it makes life much easier.

Cleaning is generally performed using a mild detergent of some sort, either a specialist cleaning product such as Bruclean, or a household product such as Oxi or bleach. There is no need to use a huge amount of cleaning solution: a few litres in the bottom of a bucket and a bit of elbow grease with a foam-backed plastic scrubber or a microfibre cloth is usually enough. Any areas that look dirty must be scrubbed clean, but ensuring that all the surfaces are wetted by the solution and given a bit of a scrub is all that is necessary for ordinary cleaning duties. Badly soiled items may require a lengthy soak of up to an hour. Do not use metal scourers that will scratch the surface – the scratches can harbour bacteria.

Disinfecting

Disinfecting is the process of making your equipment microbiologically clean and entails killing the bacteria that are present on the surfaces of your equipment. The equipment must be physically clean first or the disinfecting stage can be rendered ineffective. If the disinfectant cannot get at the micro-organisms because they are buried in crud, it can't kill them, no matter how microscopic that crud may be. Prior cleanliness is particularly important when using chlorine-based disinfectant. The presence of excessive organic matter interferes with the killing power of the solution, or uses up the killing power prematurely.

Your mash tun and boiler, or anything that comes into contact with the wort before the boiling stage, does not need to be disinfected – the heat of the boil will do that – but nevertheless it does need to be clean.

The most commonly used disinfectants in brewing are usually chlorine based – either a proprietary product such as Bruclean, or ordinary household bleach. All disinfectants need a minimum contact time to be effective. This is usually 20 minutes

or so, but some disinfectants work within a couple of minutes. It is important that all surfaces are wetted, and remain wetted, during the contact period. Every ten minutes or so, simply use a cloth or foam-backed scrubber to re-wet the surfaces and give a light rub.

Buckets 'n' bins, bits 'n' bobs

As well as obvious things such as bins, lids, casks and bottles, smaller items such as hydrometers, thermometers, funnels, paddles and spoons should be cleaned and disinfected. The taps on casks and bins should frequently be removed and soaked in cleaning and disinfecting solution, as should the caps of casks. Remove sealing rings from cask caps and soak them separately. Lightly smear with petroleum jelly (Vaseline) before reassembling. Safety valves on caps should also not be forgotten. Pay attention to siphon tubing – it should be thoroughly cleaned and disinfected both inside and out.

Bottles

Cleaning, disinfecting and rinsing 40 pint bottles is a tedious chore but if you like to hold a wide range of beers in stock, it is a necessary evil. There is no really easy way to do it. I usually clean my bottles in batches by soaking them in a bin of cleaner. They are then rinsed and soaked in a bin of disinfectant, then rinsed again. Large, stackable, rectangular plastic storage bins make good vessels to soak bottles in. They can also be used to store bottles afterwards. You can ensure that the bottles are full of cleaner/disinfectant during the soak by standing them upright, which is why a rectangular bin works best. If the bottles need a brush, use the brush while the bottle is submerged to prevent cleaner spraying everywhere – your eyes in particular.

Heavily soiled bottles require more thorough treatment. I usually fill up the bottles with strong cleaner using a funnel and leave them to stand for a while. A few grains of rice added to the bottle along with the detergent, and swirled around, does a remarkably good job of loosening stubborn deposits. A bottle stand to aid draining is useful.

Cleaning and disinfectant products

All cleaners and disinfectants are hazardous by nature, particularly in their concentrated form, and have unpleasant consequences if misused. Adequate precautions must be taken to protect yourself and those around you. At the very least I recommend eye protection and protective gloves. Sensible precautions include not creating or inhaling the dust of powdered products and not splashing liquids about. Always use in well ventilated areas.

Many disinfectants are based on a bleach of one form or another, usually chlorine, and the product will do exactly that – it will bleach. It can damage work tops, floor tiles, carpets, your clothes and anything else it comes into contact with. Some disinfectants are acidic and can burn. Always keep the tops on bottles when not using them.

Never mix different cleaners together indiscriminately. Not only is there the possibility that you will neutralise the whole cocktail, rendering it ineffective, but combining some chemicals, such as ammonia-based products with chlorine-based products, will produce a toxic gas that is not far removed from the stuff that the Germans and British were lobbing at each other during the First World War.

Always check that the cleaner or disinfectant you propose to use is compatible with any metals in your set up. Aluminium equipment in particular is not compatible with most common cleaning products. Always read the safety information on the packaging. Most products in their diluted form are relatively safe if used properly, but they can still damage the eyes and irritate or degrease the skin, so never take safety for granted.

Bruclean

Bruclean, distributed by Brupaks, is a powdered combined cleaner/ disinfectant. Bruclean is one of the few products that is safe on aluminium, but nevertheless it should not be left in prolonged contact with metals of any sort. It is generally used at a solution of 5 to 10 grams per litre and can be used hot or cold. Contact time is 15 to 20 minutes. The product should be adequately rinsed afterwards. Read the label before use.

Soda crystals, sodium carbonate

Soda crystals, otherwise known as washing soda or sodium carbonate, is an inexpensive but often overlooked and underrated cleaner and degreaser. It can be found in the washing powder section of all major supermarkets. It has to be used in fairly high concentrations compared to some other cleaners, not least because the crystals contain 63% water, but despite that it still works out an inexpensive cleaner. It is not a bad idea to add a small squirt of washing-up liquid to a soda crystal solution to act as a wetting agent and thus improve its effectiveness. In common with most cleaning products, soda crystal solutions are more effective when dissolved in hot water.

The concentration of soda crystal used in solutions for heavy-duty cleaning purposes is usually fairly high, but it is only if you have neglected your equipment that a high concentration is necessary. You shouldn't need to use more than one or two tablespoonfuls of soda crystals per litre unless you have long-term dried-on deposits to remove. There is no need to make up more than a litre or two of solution at a time unless you have a large number of bits and bobs that you need to soak. Contact time for a soda crystal solution should be about 20 minutes, with the occasional use of elbow grease and re-wetting the surfaces every ten minutes or so. Cleaned items must be rinsed very thoroughly afterwards. Never use soda crystals on aluminium.

Sodium percarbonate (Oxi or Oxy)

This is a combined cleaner and moderate disinfectant in powder form that can be regarded as turbocharged soda crystals. It contains a sodium carbonate-type base and a hydrogen-peroxide bleach, releasing something the makers call active oxygen when in solution. It is used as a laundry bleach/stain remover and can be found in supermarkets as well as home-brewing shops.

This is remarkably effective stuff at cleaning; much better than ordinary soda crystals. The plain stuff without optical brighteners and perfumes, such as Wizz Oxi Ultra, is all you need.

Normal concentration is about eight grams per litre of hot water and twice that amount for heavy-duty cleaning. The domestic variants are usually supplied with a 25 ml measuring scoop which gives a convenient measure of one scoop per 5 litres or around one scoop per gallon. Contact time is usually five to ten minutes, but up to around 20 minutes for heavily soiled equipment. Rinse well afterwards.

The solution is only fully effective for a short time because when all the available oxygen has effervesced away, the resultant stuff is no more powerful than ordinary washing soda. Do not store the solution in a sealed container such as a spray bottle because the solution effervesces and will pressurise the bottle – at best it will leak and at worst it will explode. Do not use on aluminium.

Household bleach, sodium hypochlorite

Household bleach has faithfully served the home-brewing hobby for many years. It is made from sodium hypochlorite with added sodium hydroxide (caustic soda) as a pH adjuster/stabiliser. At high concentrations it has good cleaning properties and at low concentrations it has excellent disinfecting properties. Sodium hypochlorite bleach has been one of society's most potent weapons against a wide array of life-threatening infections for more than 160 years. Domestic bleach kills the widest range of pathogens of any inexpensive disinfectant and it is extremely powerful against viruses, bacteria and spores at room temperature. Nothing beats it and there are very few modern disinfectants that come anywhere near even to equalling it. This stuff is so powerful and so cheap that I can see little point in using anything else for disinfecting.

For cleaning heavily contaminated equipment including beer bottles and or casks, a 5 per cent solution (50 ml per litre – one volume of bleach made up to 20 volumes by adding 19 volumes of water) is typical, but

one to two per cent is more than adequate for normal cleaning. A much lower concentration is fine for light disinfecting duty.

Selecting bleach

Supermarkets sell the well-known named brands of bleach, their own-brand versions and often a 'value' version as well. In addition bleach comes in thick and thin varieties. The strength of bleach varies enormously between brands, but the concentration of these bleaches is rarely printed on the container.

Thick bleaches have thickeners in them to make them cling to surfaces better, but they also have surfactants to enhance their cleaning power and often an added perfume. The thickeners are there to resist rinsing and the surfactants greatly enhance cleaning performance. Thin bleaches usually have none of the above. They are just sodium hypochlorite with a bit of sodium hydroxide if you are lucky.

One of the very few bleaches that actually has the strength specified on the bottle is Domestos, which states 4.9% w/w sodium hypochlorite. I am aware that one supermarket own-brand bleach contains just 1.8% sodium hypochlorite, and many thin bleaches, whether value or otherwise, contain just 1.1% sodium hypochlorite – 22 per cent of the strength of thick bleach. Therefore it is safest to assume that all thin and value bleaches will be around 1.1%, and some own-brands may be even less than that. So you will need four and a

BLEACH CONCENTRATIONS

Application	Chlorine required	Standard bleach	Value bleach
Heavy-duty cleaning	2700 ppm	60 ml/l	270 ml/l
Medium-duty cleaning	1125 ppm	25 ml/l	112 ml/l
Light-duty cleaning	540 ppm	12 ml/l	55 ml/l
Standard disinfectant	200 ppm	4.5 ml/l	20 ml/l

Multiply the quantity by the required volume of your cleaning solution, in litres, to arrive at the quantity of bleach to be added. For example: to make 5 litres of standard disinfectant, 22.5 ml of standard bleach should be added to 5 litres of water. Alternatively, 275 ml of cheap or value bleach is needed in 5 litres of water to make a light-duty cleaner.

half times the quantity of thin bleach to do the same job as thick bleach.

Some home-brewers prefer to use thin bleaches on the basis of perceived easier rinsing and lack of perfume. However, I prefer the security of knowing the strength of the bleach so that I am assured that my cleaning and disinfecting solutions are of adequate strength. For home-brewing purposes I use Domestos Original bleach (which does not come in a thin version). The thickeners are not really an issue in the low concentrations and high dilution rates that we use. Thorough rinsing is obviously required, but you need to do that anyway.

Using bleach

The articles to be cleaned or disinfected should be immersed in or thoroughly wetted with the solution for about 20 minutes, brushed, then thoroughly rinsed afterwards. It is important to remove all traces of the chlorine that might otherwise taint the finished beer.

Metals or glassware should not be left in contact with the bleach solution for extended periods because the bleach can cause corrosion on metal and produce a frosted effect on glass. Always stick to the minimum contact time necessary to do the job. Do not store items away with bleach in them or on them. The diluted solution will not keep for any length of time, a few hours at most.

SAFETY ADVICE

✓ *Use bleach in a well-ventilated area.*

✓ *Wear eye protection and protective gloves.*

✗ *Bleach is caustic and is therefore quite nasty undiluted – take care.*

✗ *Bleach is unsuitable for use on aluminium or zinc.*

✗ *Never mix bleach with ammonia compounds or other cleaners – toxic gases will be generated.*

✗ *Do not mix with acids – chlorine gas could be liberated.*

✗ *Do not use in concentrated form, always dilute with water.*

✓ *Always rinse thoroughly afterwards.*

Brewing Instructions
Malt extract beers

Those recipes that use the ingredients pale malt, crystal malt, black malt, roast barley or sugars and syrups are suitable for brewing using this simple brewing method. No mash is required – the pale malt is replaced by pale malt extract and all the ingredients are simply boiled together in the boiler.

Any type of malt extract can be used, but a fresh, pale-coloured, premium-grade malt extract syrup, otherwise known as liquid malt extract, is preferred. Dried malt extract can also be used and is in fact a better option if the freshness of the malt extract syrup cannot be guaranteed. Stale malt extract syrup or malt extract syrup that has been stored inappropriately can impart off-flavours – the well-known malt extract 'tang'. Dried malt extract has a much longer shelf life and is easier to store and handle.

The recipes in this book that are suitable for malt extract brewing specify at the bottom the quantity of malt extract to use. Simply omit any pale malt, mild ale malt or amber malt called for in the recipe and replace it with the quantity of light-coloured malt extract specified.

Generally speaking, malt extract beers do not neet water treatment because the critical mashing stage has already been done (see *p47*).

Preparation

If necessary, make up a yeast starter solution two or three days before you intend to brew (see p33).

Stand the container of malt extract syrup in hot water for five or ten minutes prior to brewing in order to soften it.

The boil

Put about 18 litres of water (liquor) into the boiler and heat to about 40°C. Stir in the malt extract and any grains, but not the sugars or hops. The heat source should be turned off while the malt extract is stirred in to prevent it scorching on the heater before it has properly dissolved. When the extract has fully dissolved, top up the boiler with water to a volume as near to the final volume as can be achieved, remembering to leave sufficient headroom for the foam produced during boiling. Turn on the heat and bring to the boil.

Some brewers object to boiling the grains on the grounds that it could introduce grainy off-tastes. This is not a real problem in my view, but an alternative is to put the grains into some sort of muslin bag and put it in the boiler along with the malt extract at 40°C, then fish the bag out just before the wort comes to the boil.

Add the first batch of hops as soon the wort comes to the boil, and add any sugars or syrups halfway through. A good, vigorous boil for a period of about one and a half hours is required.

Ten minutes before the end of the boiling period, add the second batch of hops and the Irish moss.

Irish moss helps to precipitate haze-forming proteins out of the wort, but there is little benefit to be gained from using it when brewing dark beers. When the wort has boiled for the desired length of time, switch off the boiler and allow time for the trub and hop debris to settle. If you are adding post-boil hops, wait for the temperature to drop somewhat – around 80°C is regarded as optimum – and stir in your hops.

Run the wort into a collection vessel, taking care to ensure that as much debris as possible is left behind in the boiler, filtered by the bed of hops. If the first runnings are full of sediment they should be returned to the boiler for refiltering.

Wort cooling

The process from here onwards is common to all beers. Continue from the heading Wort cooling on p76.

Full mash beers

All of the recipes in this book are primarily designed for brewing from grain using the full mash technique. Full mashing is the best method for getting close to emulating the commercial beer recipes in these pages. Mashing produces distinctive, quality beers, and is the only technique that gives the brewer complete and flexible control over his product.

Preparation

If necessary, make up a yeast starter solution a couple of days before you intend to brew (see *p33*). If you treat your water by boiling, perform the water treatment the evening before you brew and store it ready for use (see *p40*).

All of the malted grains used in making ale need to be crushed before they can be successfully mashed. Crushing the malt is a difficult process to perform without proper equipment. Home-brewing shops can supply the stuff already crushed and unless you have a grain mill you should purchase it in this form. Cereal adjuncts such as flaked maize and torrefied barley do not need to be crushed.

Mash liquor

Put 25 litres of treated water (liquor) into the brewing boiler or hot liquor tank and heat it to around 80°C. When the liquor is up to temperature run the specified volume of into the mash tun.

Put the lid on the tun and wait a few minutes for it to preheat and the temperature of the mash liquor to stabilise. Allow the temperature to reduce to strike heat (about 72°C), either by waiting for the temperature to fall naturally or by adding incremental amounts of cold liquor. Stir the mash liquor from time to time to equalise the temperature. Adjust the temperature if necessary by adding boiling or cold liquor.

The mash

When you have assured yourself that the temperature of the mash liquor is at strike heat, carefully add the grist and stir it into the liquor to form a thick porridge-like mass. Stir thoroughly to ensure that there are no dry pockets remaining or an inefficient mash will result. However, take care not to over-stir or the grain will become waterlogged – air in the grain will be expelled and the goods will lose their buoyancy and pack down onto the false bottom of the tun. This can cause a set mash, making draining the tun very difficult, and efficiency will suffer because the mash liquor cannot freely percolate through a compacted mass of grain.

The act of adding the grain to the hot liquor should lower the temperature of the mass to approximately the correct mashing temperature – around 66°C. Make any final adjustments to the temperature by adding boiling or cold liquor and rapidly stirring it well into the mash. Keep careful notes of strike water temperature and mash temperature, and you can compensate for any discrepancies next time you mash by adjusting the strike heat accordingly.

Then fit the lid, cover it with heavy thermal insulation and leave the tun undisturbed for the mashing period. Do not keep removing the lid to measure temperature or pH for example, because excessive heat loss will occur. It is better to measure the temperature at the end of the mash if you wish to discover how well your tun retains its heat.

A typical mash period is 90 minutes. Some home-brewers reduce this to 60 minutes to save time, but a lower quality wort or a poorly-balanced wort is likely to result, particularly if the temperature of the mash drops significantly during the mash period. Lower temperatures generally require longer mash times.

While the mash is in progress ensure that there is sufficient treated water in the boiler or hot liquor tank for sparging, and set it to maintain the sparge liquor at a temperature of about 85°C.

Sparging

When the mash has finished steeping, it is time to start collection and sparging. The exact mechanics of this operation depend upon equipment available, the effort you are willing to expend on sparging and other personal preferences. Sparging is performed by rinsing the grains with treated hot water maintained at a temperature of about 80°C to flush out the sugars that are trapped in the grains.

In an ideal situation, sparging is initiated first and then run-off is started, and the inflow of sparge liquor is matched by the run-off of sweet wort such that the grains remain floating and do not compact down onto the false bottom and block it – a situation known as a set mash. The sparge should be very slow for optimum efficiency, and the temperature of the sparge liquor should be such that the temperature of the grain bed and the outflow of the sweet wort rises to about 76°C.

Usually we sparge with water at 80 to 85°C. This temperature reduces wort viscosity which aids mash tun run-off, and arrests beta-amylase activity but permits alpha-amylase activity. This holds the sugar profile in balance, preventing too much of the non-fermentable sugar from being converted into fermentable sugar which would otherwise produce an overly dry beer (unless that is what is intended). By permitting the alpha-amylase to work, undegraded starch is converted into sugar, preventing a haze from forming in the beer.

Ideally, the sparge should be a light spray, as fine as drizzle, to ensure that the mash bed does not crack. Jugging hot water over the surface of the mash is a popular method of sparging, but care must be taken not to disturb the grain bed too much.

The grain should act as a filter-bed and filter the wort bright. The first runnings may be full of sediment; these are usually returned to the mash tun until it runs bright.

Stop sparging when the gravity of the spargings falls to below about 1008 or when sufficient wort has been collected. With experience you will not need to measure the gravity – you can determine when to stop by tasting the wort. If it is sweet, goodness is still being extracted, so continue. If it tastes like water, it probably is, so it's about the right time to stop. If it tastes bitter, astringent or tannic (like stewed tea), then definitely stop. Usually you will have collected a boiler full of wort before any problems emerge.

A simple method of sparging that does not require additional equipment is re-mashing – this is what the commercial brewers used to do before rotating sparge arms were invented. Run off the mash tun and when it has drained close the tap and gently recharge the mash tun with water at about 80°C. Stir thoroughly and leave to stand for 15 to 30 minutes. After the standing period run off the mash tun as before. Repeat this operation once more if necessary, gauging the quantity of water added so that the proper volume is collected.

The boil

Once the wort has been collected, top up the boiler with treated water to a volume as near to the final volume as can be achieved, remembering to leave sufficient headroom to accommodate the foam produced during boiling.

Add the first batch of hops as soon the wort comes to the boil, and add any sugars or syrups about halfway through. A good, vigorous boil for a period of around 90 minutes is required. About ten minutes before the end of the boiling period, add the second batch of hops and the Irish moss. Irish moss helps to precipitate haze-forming proteins out of the wort, but there is little benefit to be gained from using it when brewing dark beers. When the wort has boiled for the desired length of time, switch off the boiler and allow time for the trub and hop debris to settle. If post-boil hops are being added, wait for the temperature to drop – 80°C is the optimum – and stir in your hops.

Run the wort into a collection vessel, taking care to ensure that as much debris as possible is left behind in the boiler, filtered by the bed of hops. If the first runnings are full of sediment they should be returned to the boiler for refiltering.

Fermentation and finishing

Wort cooling

The next stage is wort cooling. The wort must be cooled to below 30°C before it is safe to pitch the yeast. It will take several hours for the wort to cool down naturally – in the absence of cooling equipment, simply fit the lid to your bin and leave the wort to cool overnight.

Forced cooling allows us to get on with the job more quickly and reduces the possibility of infection by bacteria. Some home-brewers cool by standing the bin of hot wort in a slightly larger vessel containing cold water. The kitchen sink, an old tin bath or even the domestic bath can be used. As long as the hot wort is stirred regularly to equalise the temperature, and the cold water is changed as it heats up, the cooling water does not need to come very far up the side of the bin. This method, though quicker than doing nothing, is still fairly inefficient because the plastic bin does not transfer heat very well. Lugging 23 litres of hot liquid about is a hazardous business too.

The most efficient cooling method is to employ an immersion cooler – a copper cooling coil through which cold water is passed (see p58 for more information). In this case cooling is often performed in the boiler before the wort is run off.

Wort aeration

After cooling, the wort is adjusted to the correct specific gravity by adding cold water, then it is aerated. Yeast needs a certain amount of dissolved air to be present in the wort at the start of fermentation in order to multiply and establish itself. The wort boil drives off all the air, so it is important to put some back. This can be acheived by pouring the wort vigorously from one bin to another, generating lots of swirling motion and plenty of mechanical action. Alternatively, running the wort slowly from one bin to another through the tap is all that is required. In this case just one transfer would be sufficient. The most efficient method is to whisk the wort using a brewer's paddle powered by a cordless drill.

Fermentation

Ensure that the temperature of the wort is below 30°C before the yeast is pitched. Add the contents of the yeast starter bottle, or rehydrated yeast, to the wort and fermentation begins. Stand the fermentation vessel in a convenient place where the temperature can be maintained between about 18°C and 22°C, ideally at 20°C. The lid can be fitted to the bin until the yeast head has begun to form, then removed. When the head has established itself the surface will contain some dark floccules and trub brought up with the yeast. These should be skimmed off, taking care to cause the minimum of disturbance to the rest of the head.

Many home-brewing books recommend frequent yeast skimming. I do not go along with this. I do not believe in continually interfering with the ale. The only time that I skim yeast is if it is in danger of spilling over the sides of the bin, if it has undesirable things on the surface, or if it is in danger of collapsing into the ale at the end of fermentation. While the yeast is sitting on top of the ale it is protecting it from airborne bacteria, and that is why open-fermented ales use top-working yeasts.

You will have to make up your own mind on the pros and cons of yeast skimming. With some yeasts of course, no skimming is required, because the yeast sits on the bottom. In the case of bottom workers, or if the surface of the beer becomes exposed, fit the lid loosely to the bin.

Fermentation is deemed to be complete when the specific gravity has remained static for 24 hours and is somewhere close to the quoted final gravity. Remember that the final gravity is only given as a guide. It is unlikely to be spot on.

Casking

When fermentation has stopped, or when the specific gravity has fallen close to final gravity, it is time for casking. I usually transfer my ale to an intermediate vessel first, fit the lid and leave it to stand in a cool place for a couple of days in an attempt to encourage more yeast to settle out. However this is not essential and many home-brewers do not bother.

Transfer of the beer from fermentation vessel to cask can be performed using a siphon. Care must be taken to ensure that a minimum amount of air comes into contact with the beer – make sure that the outlet end of the tube remains submerged in the beer being transferred. Take care not to transfer sediment. If you transfer your beer to cask using the tap on your fermenter, you should attach some tubing to it and keep the outlet end under the surface of the beer to prevent excessive air ingestion. Ideally the casks should be filled quite full, but that is often difficult to achieve with the size of casks currently available to us. The cask should then be stowed away and the ale matured for an appropriate period.

If the cask has a large amount of air space remaining, the air should be expelled by carefully releasing and re-sealing the cap after two or three days, and then again a day or two later. It may also be beneficial to add about 50 grams of cane sugar or 80 grams of malt extract primings at the time of filling to generate conditioning gas rapidly.

Maturation

The stronger the beer, the longer the maturation period should be. Weak beers benefit from a minimum of a couple of weeks; strong beers, a month or more. Not many commercial brewers mature their beers for any length of time these days, but almost any beer will benefit from an extended period of maturation. As a general rule allow one week for every 10° of gravity – so four weeks should be allowed for a beer with an original gravity of1040. The weakest beers will keep for at least three months and the strongest several years.

Bottling

All beer destined for bottling should first be matured for a time in a cask. Bottling straight from the fermentation vessel is bad practice and should be avoided. A bottle is a tightly sealed container, and the volatile products of fermentation have no way of escape. Even the worst commercial breweries mature their bottled beers in a conditioning tank before bottling. Ordinary beers will need a week or two in cask, strong beers up to a month – very strong beers for as long as your patience lasts. The ideal time to bottle is just at the point that the ale would be ready for drinking if it was to be a cask ale.

The cask should be vented by releasing the cap slightly a day or so before bottling is to begin and the beer should have dropped bright before bottling is attempted. The bottles should be filled by means of a siphon tube that reaches to the bottom of the bottle, taking care that a minimum of air is absorbed. When filling, leave about half an inch

of space in the neck of the bottle. The crown caps should be sterilised in a proprietary cleaner or boiling water before use. It will take about six weeks for the bottles to come into condition. The bottles should be stored for a minimum of a month, preferably longer.

You would not go far wrong by following Bass's instructions from the 19th century:

BASS'S BOTTLING INSTRUCTIONS (1880)

1 *Ale should not be bottled during summer, or in warm weather. Home bottling should be completed by the end of June at the latest. Summer-brewed ale should, however, be bottled as soon as it gets into condition.*

2 *When ale is received, it should be at once placed bung upwards on the scantling in the cellar, so as to allow the porous spiles to work; when thus placed it must be left undisturbed.*

3 *Each cask is usually provided with one or more porous pegs in the bung, which will carry off the gas generated by fermentation. It will only be necessary to make any alteration with regard to these pegs in the case of their having become so much clogged that the cask would burst if the requisite vent were not given; or in the opposite case of a tendency in the beer to become flat, when hard spiles must be substituted.*

4 The cellar ought to be well ventilated, kept perfectly clean, and as cool as possible. Underground cellars are usually the best.

5 Immediately the beer is bright and sparkling, and in a quiet state, it is in the proper condition to be bottled.

6 If from any cause the ale should not become fit for bottling in the usual time, it will generally be sufficient to pass it through the grounds again; i.e., roll it over and put it up again on the scantling.

7 Ordinary bottling taps, with long tubes reaching almost to the bottom of the bottles, are recommended. All taps, pipes and vessels used for ale should be kept scrupulously clean.

8 The bottles when filled should be corked without delay.

9 The bottles should be piled standing upright. Should the ale be sluggish in ripening, the bottles may be laid down, but this is seldom necessary.

10 Bottled ale is never fit to be sent out under a month. It takes at least that time to acquire the bottled flavour.

11 As the ale ripens in bottle a sediment is thrown down. In uncorking a bottle, therefore, be very careful to avoid disturbing this.

12 In decanting, pour out the ale in a jug, carefully keeping back the sediment within the bottle.

NB – With respect to ale consumed on draught, remarks Nos. 2 to 6 inclusive are equally applicable, always taking care to give as little vent as possible.

Fining and priming

Fining is the addition of a clearing agent, either gelatine or isinglass, which assists in clearing the beer by dragging yeast out of suspension. Priming is the practice of adding fermentable sugars to the cask in order to bring the beer rapidly into condition – to make the beer lively by encouraging further rapid fermentation that puts carbon dioxide gas into solution.

A well-brewed beer, kept its proper time, should not need priming or fining. A good yeast will clear down unaided, and residual dextrins (carbohydrates) in the beer will slowly ferment and produce perfect condition.

A home-brewer may need recourse to fining or priming under certain circumstances. A beer may not be clearing well and fining may help it along. A beer that uses a high proportion of cane sugar in its makeup may be deficient in slowly-fermenting dextrins so may need priming to help get it into condition. Also, a home-brewer may want to fine and prime for the same reason that a commercial brewery does; to get a beer into drinkable condition in the shortest possible time.

It should not be necessary to prime and fine bottled beers. The fining of bottled beers can cause loose sediment rather than a tightly-packed yeast deposit, which can make them difficult to pour.

White cane sugar can be used for priming casks if the beer is to be drunk within a short period of time. A malt extract solution is better, particularly if the beer is to be kept longer. In each case, 50-80 grams, made into a syrup with about 250 ml of boiling water, will do the trick for a 23-litre batch. Keep the solution covered and allow it to cool.

Isinglass finings are discussed on *p38*. The finings should be mixed with a small quantity of beer before adding them to the cask. They are best added a day or two after casking, preferably longer. Finings will not work properly if the yeast is still active and not ready to drop. Good quality isinglass finings will fine a beer within about 12 hours of being added.

Hints and Tips

● If you brew during the summer months, the chances of infection from airborne wild yeasts and bacteria are much higher. It is safest to brew between October and April.

● Make a to-do list before you start your brewing session. It is easy to forget things you will need such as water treatment salts, Irish moss and the like.

● Keep accurate records of everything: temperatures, dates, times, quantities.

● Give each brewing session a reference number that is easy to decipher and put that in your records and on your casks or bottles. When you examine your stock you will be able to tell at a glance how old a beer is and consume it in proper rotation.

● Ensure that everything that comes into contact with your wort or beer after the boiling stage is thoroughly clean and disinfected before use.

● Stand your vessels and your boiler on towels to make cleaning up after accidental boil-overs easier. Your fermenter should also have a plastic sheet underneath as it's not unusual for a vigorous yeast head to overspill the vessel.

● Aerate the wort before or just after pitching the yeast by vigorously stirring for five minutes. The most efficient way to whisk is to use a brewer's paddle fitted into a cordless electric drill.

● It is a good idea to give the wort another thorough aeration 24 hours or so after fermentation has begun.

● You may need to aerate the wort further during fermentation, particularly when brewing a strong beer and certainly if fermentation has stuck. However, it is important not to allow air into the beer at any time close to completion of fermentation or after it is complete.

● Always have a spare sachet or two of a reliable yeast handy to use in an emergency. Something like Safale-04 is recommended.

● Rehydrating a yeast in water that is too hot will kill the yeast. Yeast should be hydrated in water at 30-35°C, never any warmer.

● Yeast can be stunned by sudden temperature changes either during hydration, pitching or fermentation. Never subject the yeast to sudden temperature changes greater than about 10°C. Allow the yeast to acclimatise to ambient before rehydrating, and the beer and yeast slurry to be within 10°C or so of each other before pitching.

● Ensure that the wort is below 30°C before pitching the yeast.

● Primary fermentation is complete when the specific gravity reading remains static for a period of 24 hours and is close to the predicted final gravity.

● The specified final gravity in the recipes is a an approximation. Actual final gravity depends on many things, particularly the yeast strain employed. The specified final gravity should be considered the minimum likely to be achieved. If you are within a few points of it, and the specific gravity reading remains stable for 24 hours, you are near enough.

● A stuck fermentation is indicated if activity slows and the specific gravity remains static, well above the predicted final gravity. A stuck fermentation can usually be restored by rousing (stirring to re-suspend the yeast) and, in some cases, re-aeration.

● Leaving beer in the primary fermenter for two or three days after primary fermentation will improve the flavour and reduce sediment in the cask or bottle.

● When transferring beer to cask or bottle, ensure that as little air as possible is absorbed during the transfer. To do this use a length of

plastic syphon tubing with some rigid tubing on the end (preferably on both ends) so that the outlet of the tube remains submerged under the surface of the beer at all times.

● Beer should be matured for at least two weeks. As a rule of thumb give a maturation period of one week for every ten degrees of original gravity above 1000. A 1040 beer would be optimum at four weeks.

● Bottled beers can take six weeks or more to come into condition after bottling.

● If you wish to prime bottled beers, do not stir the primings into the cask or fermenter – this will disturb the yeast sediment causing cloudy beer and excessive sediment in the bottles. It is better to tip your finings into the bottom of a clean and sterilised bin and syphon the beer from the cask or fermenter onto this. This will ensure reasonably good mixing without getting much air into solution or creating sediment. Bottle from this secondary vessel.Alternatively, make up 250 ml of priming solution using 80 grams of sugar or malt extract for 23/25 litres and add 5 ml of this solution to each bottle before filling, using a medicine syringe obtainable from pharmacists.

● When serving beer from a bottom-tap cask, don't allow a vacuum to form in the cask as the beer is delivered. This will cause a large bubble of air to be drawn in through the tap which will stir up the yeast and produce a cloudy beer. If you sense this happening by the flow slowing, close the tap and either crack open the cap gently to admit some air, or give the cask a quick burst with your gas injector.

Safe technique

Home-brewing entails much transferring of liquid from one vessel to another. A full brewing bin weighs about 25 kg – a fair weight to lift when that weight includes a fluid that sloshes around with a will of its own, making the operation unstable and difficult to control.

Furthermore there is the boiling phase in beer production – boiling liquids are dangerous to move, particularly in plastic bins which tend to soften when hot. The fitted handles are of dubious strength and it would be folly to rely on them.

Safe technique requires a system that minimises the lifting of fluids and eliminates the necessity to move hot fluids. For this to be accomplished without the aid of pumps, a multilevel system is required. Most of us have just a worktop or bench and the floor to work with, but a three-level system can be fabricated using a worktop.

A simple system is described below. It assumes that the boiler also doubles as a hot liquor tank. If you have a separate hot liquor tank you will have to modify the procedure accordingly. It also assumes that you have a couple of largish jugs – the larger the better.

The boiler is situated on the worktop. Below that, sitting on a chair or something else of appropriate height

that is stable and safe, is the mash tun, and on the floor is a collection vessel of some sort, usually a standard bin. The hot liquor tank commands the mash tun and the mash tun commands the collection vessel.

Everything is straightforward until the sparging operation and it is at this point that the jiggery-pokery begins. During sparging. the run-off is run into the collection vessel until it is about half full. The sparge is then stopped and the collection vessel moved to the worktop – at this point it is easier to lift and unlikely to splash uncontrollably. The sparge is then resumed and the run-off collected in jugs that are emptied into the collection vessel. If you are sparging by pouring jugs full of hot water over the mash, the system is simplified further because the mash tun can be situated on the worktop.

When sufficient wort has been collected the boiler is moved down a level onto the chair and the collected wort run into it. The boil then commences.

After the boil and any late hopping additions, the wort is cooled. If you have an immersion cooler, the wort is cooled in-situ in the boiler before running into the fermenting bin. Otherwise the hot wort is run into the fermenting bin, the lid fitted, and it is left to cool to a safe temperature before attempting to move it. It is then allowed to cool naturally to pitching temperature.

The only full-weight lift necessary with this system is moving the fermented beer to a higher level to cask or bottle it, and you can get someone to assist you with that.

About the Recipes

The recipes in this book are not necessarily exact replicas of commercial breweries' recipes because, often, although the ingredients are known, the exact ratios are not and these have been derived empirically. Some recipes have been reformulated to use more easily obtainable ingredients.

Volume

All the recipes in this book are given in three volumes to account for the different sizes of brewing bin and cask commonly available to home-brewers: 19 litres, 23 litres and 25 litres. It is easy to convert from one volume to another by dividing the required volume by recipe volume to come up with a factor, and then multiply all the ingredients by that factor. For example, if you want to brew 30 litres and the recipe is for 23 litres: 30 divided by 23 equals 1.3. Multiply all the ingredients including hops by 1.3.

All volumes are given in litres. Conversion tables are provided on *p200* for home-brewers using other measuring systems.

The recipes assume an overall efficiency of 75 per cent. This is fairly conservative and most brewers should be able to exceed this figure and end up with the specified gravity of beer at the specified volume.

Original gravity

This is the original gravity quoted by the brewery, where available. The recipes are designed to match this gravity. When the true original gravity is not known it has been reverse-engineered and calculated from the alcohol figure.

Ingredients

The ingredients specified are usually those that have been specified by the brewer. Some of the recipes have been reformulated to use more easily available ingredients. The most common change is to substitute ordinary white cane sugar where invert sugar is used by the brewery.

In many cases a small amount of black malt has been added to adjust for colour when the brewery obviously uses added caramel or dark invert sugar. You can safely omit small quantities of black malt if you are not too fussy about matching colour. It is a very woolly approximation anyway.

The type of barley malt used by the brewery has not been specified in the recipes. It might make a small difference to the flavour, but not to the success of the recipe. A great many breweries claim to use Maris Otter pale malt, but this seems to me to have parallels with the Beaujolais Nouveau wine conundrum, where much more wine is produced than would account for the entire annual grape harvest of the region. I am sure that there is not enough Maris Otter grown to supply all the breweries that claim to use it, and I treat most claims with suspicion.

The same could also be said about the number of breweries claiming to use Fuggles and Goldings hops. However, unlike the barley, hop varieties do make a substantial difference to flavour so where a brewer claims to use them, they have been specified, even though I do not necessarily believe it.

Total liquor

An attempt to give an indication of the total amount of liquor (water) to be treated prior to a brewing session. Note that some fixed assumptions on grain absorption and similar things have been made.

Mash liquor

Estimated quantity of mash liquor required based on 2.5 litres of liquor per kilogram of grist.

Mash temperature

In all cases it is guessed but most brewers aim for about 66°C unless they are brewing something really special. If you maintain your mash temperature between about 62°C and 68°C you will get good results.

Mash time

Mash time has been standardised at one and a half hours.

Boil time

This again has been standardised, usually at one and a half hours, although with one or two of the stronger beers two hours has been specified. A minimum of one and a half hours is required to achieve the calculated hop extraction efficiency and this length of time was assumed when calculating the weight of hops required.

Final gravity

This is provided to give some idea of how far the beer will ferment. It gives the approximate gravity at which active fermentation should finish, at which time the beer should be transferred to a cask. However, it is only an approximate figure; there are far too many variables for it to be given with any accuracy. Use your own experience to determine when primary fermentation is over.

Alcohol content

A calculated estimate of alcohol content, given as alcohol by volume (ABV).

Bitterness

In EBUs – the same as IBUs and the international standard method of assessing bitterness in beers. The bitterness figures of many of the commercial beers in this book are known, and these have been used to calculate the quantity of hops required.

Colour

The predicted colour of the beer is given in EBC. In most beers a small quantity of black malt has been used to adjust colour where the ingredients specified by the brewery do not match the specified colour. You can omit the small quantities of black malt if you wish to without affecting the overall quality of the beer.

Malt extract versions

Malt extract versions of many of the beers are given as a footnote to the main recipes. Simply replace the pale, amber or mild ale malt with the amount of extract given in the footnote appropriate to the volume being brewed. Pale coloured malt extract should be used in all cases – the beer colour is supplied by other ingredients in the recipe. Versions are given for both malt extract syrup and dried malt extract.

KEY

 Award-wining beer ★ New entry

N.B. Award winning beers are those which have been finalists in CAMRA's Champion Beer of Britain or Champion Winter Beer of Britain awards, or finalists in their respective classes. New entries are recipes that are new to the 3rd edition of *Brew Your Own British Real Ale*.

Mild Ale Recipes

A good, well-brewed Mild ale is a superb drink and was England's most popular beer, particularly among working people, until just after the Second World War. Its popularity waned from then on, partly because the brewers insisted on progressively weakening the product or faking it by merely adding caramel to their running light ales, and partly because a cloth-cap stigma became attached to the drinking of dark beers.

The term 'Mild ale' originally meant new, fresh or unmatured ale, in just the same way that we have mild or mature versions of cheeses today; the term had nothing to do with strength or colour. Like modern-day cheeses, Mild was considerably cheaper than mature beer because the expensive maturation period was absent. This cheapness encouraged people to drink it and eventually Mild became a price-driven commodity. In modern times, the term Mild has come to mean lightly hopped, or not bitter, although the price-driven argument is still present.

The popularity of Mild stems from the early days of commercial brewing. In those days, high-quality beers were matured for long periods of time; a year at least, but often considerably longer. This tied up huge amounts of capital because a whole year's supply of beer had to be brewed and stored. Considering that excise duty was paid upfront, this was an expensive undertaking that most brewers could not afford.

A new trade sprang up to accommodate this: some wealthy people made a trade of buying Mild and keeping it until it was 'stale' (mature); then selling it to the publicans at a profit. Stale was therefore more expensive than Mild – more than twice the price – so many people drank Mild and this eventually came to dominate public taste. Mixing Mild with a small quantity of stale beer was a way of producing a more palatable beer at an affordable price, and this was the origin of Porter.

The Milds of 300 or so years ago were simply immature versions of the standard brown beers of the day, which were brewed using the only malt widely available: brown malt. Brown malt was kilned over a hardwood fire that smoked the malt as it dried it, giving it a smoky character. The smokiness of the malt was considered a part of the characteristic of a beer, just as peat-smoked malt is used to make the best whiskies today, although modern beer drinkers find smoked malt objectionable.

Over the centuries dark Mild has evolved into its present form. Influenced by 18th-century Porter, 19th-century tastes, and then 20th-century greed, the term 'Mild' has come to mean lightly hopped rather than unmatured. The character of a modern dark Mild is derived from the use of dark roasted malts and cereal adjuncts, giving it a luscious depth of flavour. In 1805, a Mild would have had a gravity of OG 1085. In 1871, Mild was typically brewed at OG 1070 and in 1913 at OG 1050. Alas, a modern-day Mild is about OG 1034.

Light-coloured Mild ales are 'mild' in the literal sense, they are ordinary pale ales that are mildly hopped. They are not expected to have the same depth of character as dark Mild ales.

Years ago many breweries produced a light-coloured mild ale called 'AK', but they have all forgotten why they termed it such, and there is some debate as to the origin of the term. James Herbert in *The Art of Brewing*, 1871, had this to say:

'AK ALE; This class of ales has very much come into use, mostly for private families, it being a light tonic Ale, and sent out by most brewers at one shilling per gallon. The gravity of this Ale is usually brewed at 20 lbs [OG 1056].'

At OG 1056, AK was quite a lot weaker than the dark Milds of the time which, according to the same author, were brewed at 25 lbs (OG 1070). The term AK is probably derived from 'Amber Kitchen Ale', being a cheaper quality of ale that you would supply for the refreshment of your servants, as was customary at one time.

Amber ales, dinner ales, kitchen ales, Mild ales and table beers figure strongly in 19th century brewery price lists, sometimes all at once. A remote possibility is that AK began as a blend of amber ale and keeping ale (stock ale), at a time when the blending of different ales was all part of the brewers' art. McMullen still brew a light Mild that they refer it to as AK, though it isn't brewed at OG 1056!

ARKELL'S MASH-TUN MILD

A tasty dark Mild, lightly hopped. It has full flavours of dark malt in the mouth, and a dry but creamy finish with nut and chocolate hints. A seasonal beer from Arkell's.

ORIGINAL GRAVITY

1036

	19 litres	23 litres	25 litres
Pipkin Pale Ale Malt (grams)	2020	2440	2650
Crystal Malt (grams)	800	970	1050
White Sugar (grams)	125	150	160
Chocolate Malt (grams)	120	140	150

Start of Boil

	19 litres	23 litres	25 litres
Fuggle Hops (grams)	34	41	45
Total liquor (litres)	26.3	31.9	34.6
Mash liquor (litres)	7.3	8.9	9.6

Mash schedule 67°C (153°F), 90 minutes
Boil time 90 minutes
Final gravity 1009
Alcohol content (ABV) 3.6%
Bitterness units (EBU) 24
Colour (EBC) 100

Malt extract version - Replace the pale malt with the appropriate quantity of pale-coloured, premium-grade malt extract and brew using the malt extract brewing method.

	19 litres	23 litres	25 litres
Malt Extract Syrup (grams)	1520	1840	2000
or			
Dried Malt Extract (grams)	1300	1580	1720

★
BANKS HANSON'S MILD

A mid to dark brown Mild with a
malty roast flavour and aftertaste.

ORIGINAL GRAVITY
1035

	19 litres	23 litres	25 litres
Pale Malt (grams)	2630	3190	3460
Crystal Malt (grams)	295	360	390
Black Malt (grams)	57	69	75
Start of Boil			
Fuggle Hops (grams)	17	21	23
Golding Hops (grams)	15	18	20
Total liquor (litres)	26.3	31.9	34.6
Mash liquor (litres)	7.4	9	9.7

Mash schedule 67°C (153°F), 90 minutes
Boil time 90 minutes
Final gravity 1009
Alcohol content (ABV) 3.4%
Bitterness units (EBU) 25
Colour (EBC) 50

Malt extract version - Replace the pale malt with the appropriate quantity of pale-
coloured, premium-grade malt extract and brew using the malt extract brewing method.

	19 litres	23 litres	25 litres
Malt Extract Syrup (grams)	1980	2400	2600
or			
Dried Malt Extract (grams)	2300	2060	2240

BASS MILD

Formerly Bass 4X Mild, now brewed by Coors in its Tadcaster brewery. A refreshingly simple, easy-drinking Mild. Malt in the mouth and a short, dry finish with pronounced nut character.

ORIGINAL GRAVITY
1032

	19 litres	23 litres	25 litres
Mild Ale Malt (grams)	2380	2880	3130
White Sugar (grams)	160	190	210
Black Malt (grams)	130	160	175

Start of Boil

Challenger Hops (grams)	19	23	25

Last Ten Minutes of Boil

Golding Hops (grams)	6	8	8
Total liquor (litres)	25.8	31.3	34
Mash liquor (litres)	6.2	7.6	8.2

Mash schedule 67°C (153°F), 90 minutes
Boil time 90 minutes
Final gravity 1007
Alcohol content (ABV) 3.3%
Bitterness units (EBU) 22
Colour (EBC) 74

Malt extract version - Replace the mild ale malt with the appropriate quantity of pale-coloured, premium-grade malt extract and brew using the malt extract brewing method.

	19 litres	23 litres	25 litres
Malt Extract Syrup (grams)	1790	2170	2360
or			
Dried Malt Extract (grams)	1540	1860	2030

BATEMANS DARK MILD

A fine example of a tasty, dark red Mild from Batemans' Wainfleet brewery. Pleasing chewy malt in the mouth, and a dry finish with roast malt and caramel notes.

ORIGINAL GRAVITY
1033

	19 litres	23 litres	25 litres
Maris Otter Pale Malt (grams)	2200	2660	2900
Crystal Malt (grams)	340	410	450
Black Malt (grams)	200	240	260
Flaked Wheat (grams)	105	130	140

Start of Boil

Challenger Hops (grams)	22	26	28

Last Ten Minutes of Boil

Golding Hops (grams)	7	9	9

Total liquor (litres)	26.1	31.7	34.4
Mash liquor (litres)	7.1	8.6	9.3

Mash schedule 67°C (153°F), 90 minutes
Final gravity 1011
Boil time 90 minutes
Alcohol content (ABV) 3.1%
Bitterness units (EBU) 24
Colour (EBC) 124

BELHAVEN 60/-

Excellent example of a Scottish Mild. This bitter-sweet reddish-brown beer is dominated by fruit and malt with a hint of roast and caramel, and increasing bitterness in the aftertaste, with a delicate dry finish.

ORIGINAL GRAVITY

1031

	19 litres	23 litres	25 litres
Pale Malt (grams)	2230	2700	2940
White Sugar (grams)	175	215	230
Black Malt (grams)	70	85	92
Crystal Malt (grams)	50	60	65

Start of Boil

Whitbread Golding Hops (grams)	22	26	28

Last Ten Minutes of Boil

Fuggle Hops (grams)	4	5	5
Golding Hops (grams)	3	4	4
Irish Moss (grams)	3	3	3

Total liquor (litres)	25.7	31.2	33.9
Mash liquor (litres)	5.8	7.1	7.7

Mash schedule 67°C (153°F), 90 minutes
Boil time 90 minutes
Final gravity 1006
Alcohol content (ABV) 3.3%
Bitterness units (EBU) 21
Colour (EBC) 43

Malt extract version - Replace the pale malt with the appropriate quantity of pale-coloured, premium-grade malt extract and brew using the malt extract brewing method.

	19 litres	23 litres	25 litres
Malt Extract Syrup (grams)	1750	2030	2210
or			
Dried Malt Extract (grams)	1510	1750	1900

BODDINGTONS MILD

Easy-drinking tawny Mild with good malt character, once brewed by
the now defunct Boddingtons Strangeways brewery in Manchester.
Chewy malt in the mouth, light finish with dark chocolate notes.

ORIGINAL GRAVITY
1032

	19 litres	23 litres	25 litres
Pale Malt (grams)	2330	2820	3060
Crystal Malt (grams)	280	340	370
Chocolate Malt (grams)	83	100	110
Black Malt (grams)	52	63	69
Start of Boil			
Fuggle Hops (grams)	16	20	22
Golding Hops (grams)	14	17	19
Last Ten Minutes of Boil			
Golding Hops (grams)	7	9	9
Total liquor (litres)	26.1	31.6	34.3
Mash liquor (litres)	6.8	8.3	9

Mash schedule 67°C (153°F), 90 minutes
Boil time 90 minutes
Alcohol content (ABV) 3.1%
Bitterness units (EBU) 24
Colour (EBC) 80

Malt extract version - Replace the pale malt with the appropriate quantity of pale-
coloured, premium-grade malt extract and brew using the malt extract brewing method.

	19 litres	23 litres	25 litres
Malt Extract Syrup (grams)	1750	2120	2300
or			
Dried Malt Extract (grams)	1510	1830	1980

GALE'S FESTIVAL MILD

A strong, dark Mild, made to the gravities of yesteryear, now brewed by Fuller's. Sweet and fruity aroma. Strong in fruity flavours, blackcurrants, raisins and raspberry, with bitterness and citric flavours in finish. Three times winner of the CAMRA Silver Award for Winter Beer Of Britain: 2003, 2004 and 2006.

ORIGINAL GRAVITY
1054

	19 litres	23 litres	25 litres
Pale Malt (grams)	3790	4590	4990
Black Malt (grams)	245	295	320
White Sugar (grams)	220	270	290
Crystal Malt (grams)	130	160	175
Torrefied Wheat (grams)	67	81	88
Start of Boil			
Fuggle Hops (grams)	39	47	51
Last Ten Minutes of Boil			
Fuggle Hops (grams)	13	16	17
Total liquor (litres)	27.5	33.4	36.3
Mash liquor (litres)	10.5	12.8	13.9

Mash schedule 67°C (153°F), 90 minutes
Boil time 90 minutes
Final gravity 1013
Alcohol content (ABV) 5.5%
Bitterness units (EBU) 24
Colour (EBC) 140

HIGHGATE MILD

A dark brown Black Country Mild with a good balance of malt and hops, and traces of roast flavour following a malty aroma.

ORIGINAL GRAVITY
1037

	19 litres	23 litres	25 litres
Halcyon Pale Malt (grams)	2800	3380	3680
Black Malt (grams)	120	145	160
White Sugar (grams)	105	130	140
Crystal Malt (grams)	37	45	48
Start of Boil			
Golding Hops (grams)	13	16	18
Challenger Hops (grams)	10	12	13
Total liquor (litres)	23.6	31.9	34.6
Mash liquor (litres)	7.3	8.9	9.6

Mash schedule 67°C (153°F), 90 minutes
Boil time 90 minutes
Final gravity 1009
Alcohol content (ABV) 3.7%
Bitterness units (EBU) 22
Colour (EBC) 70

Malt extract version - Replace the pale malt with the appropriate quantity of pale-coloured, premium-grade malt extract and brew using the malt extract brewing method.

	19 litres	23 litres	25 litres
Malt Extract Syrup (grams)	2100	2540	2670
or			
Dried Malt Extract (grams)	1810	2190	2380

HOLDEN'S BLACK COUNTRY MILD

A good red/brown Mild. A refreshing, light blend of roast malt, hops and fruit dominated by malt throughout. A dry hoppy finish.

ORIGINAL GRAVITY
1037

	19 litres	23 litres	25 litres
Pale Malt (grams)	2650	3200	3480
Crystal Malt (grams)	185	225	245
White Sugar (grams)	150	185	200
Black Malt (grams)	73	89	97
Start of Boil			
Fuggle Hops (grams)	31	38	41
Total liquor (litres)	26.2	31.8	34.5
Mash liquor (litres)	7.2	8.8	9.5

Mash schedule 67°C (153°F), 90 minutes
Boil time 90 minutes
Final gravity 1008
Alcohol content (ABV) 3.9%
Bitterness units (EBU) 22
Colour (EBC) 52

Malt extract version - Replace the pale malt with the appropriate quantity of pale-coloured, premium-grade malt extract and brew using the malt extract brewing method.

	19 litres	23 litres	25 litres
Malt Extract Syrup (grams)	1995	2410	2620
or			
Dried Malt Extract (grams)	1710	2070	2250

HOOK NORTON HOOKY DARK

A chestnut brown, easy-drinking Mild. A complex malt and
hop aroma give way to a well-balanced taste, leading to a
long, hoppy finish that is unusual for a Mild.

ORIGINAL GRAVITY

1031

	19 litres	23 litres	25 litres
Pale Malt (grams)	1770	2140	2330
Crystal Malt (grams)	245	300	325
White Sugar (grams)	245	300	325
Flaked Maize (grams)	145	180	195
Black Malt (grams)	64	78	85

Start of Boil

Challenger Hops (grams)	9	11	12
Fuggle Hops (grams)	7	9	10
Golding Hops (grams)	6	8	8

Post-Boil Hops

Fuggle Hops (grams)	8	9	10
Total liquor (litres)	26.1	31.7	34.4
Mash liquor (litres)	7.1	8.6	9.3

Mash schedule 67°C (153°F), 90 minutes
Boil time 90 minutes
Final gravity 1006
Alcohol content (ABV) 3.3%
Bitterness units (EBU) 21
Colour (EBC) 50

HOP BACK MILD

A fine dark Mild with exceptional hop character, from the
Hop Back Brewery in Salisbury. Rich toasted grain in the
mouth, smooth finish with hints of vanilla and hops.

ORIGINAL GRAVITY
1032

	19 litres	23 litres	25 litres
Pale Malt (grams)	2440	2950	3210
Crystal Malt (grams)	135	165	175
Chocolate Malt (grams)	87	105	110
Roasted Barley (grams)	83	100	105
Start of Boil			
Challenger Hops (grams)	22	27	29
Last Ten Minutes of Boil			
East Kent Golding Hops (grams)	7	9	10
Total liquor (litres)	26.1	31.6	34.3
Mash liquor (litres)	6.8	8.3	9

Mash schedule 67°C (153°F), 90 minutes
Boil time 90 minutes
Final gravity 1009
Alcohol content (ABV) 3.1%
Bitterness units (EBU) 25
Colour (EBC) 92

• •

Malt extract version - Replace the pale malt with the appropriate quantity of pale-
coloured, premium-grade malt extract and brew using the malt extract brewing method.

	19 litres	23 litres	25 litres
Malt Extract Syrup (grams)	1840	2220	2420
or			
Dried Malt Extract (grams)	1580	1910	2010

HYDES DARK MILD

Dark brown/red in colour with a fruit and malt nose. Complex taste, including berry fruits, malt and a hint of chocolate. Satisfying aftertaste.

ORIGINAL GRAVITY
1034

	19 litres	23 litres	25 litres
Pale Malt (grams)	2480	3000	3260
Crystal Malt (grams)	290	350	380
Chocolate Malt (grams)	145	175	190

Start of Boil

	19 litres	23 litres	25 litres
Fuggle Hops (grams)	29	35	38

Post-Boil Hops

	19 litres	23 litres	25 litres
Fuggle Hops (grams)	6	7	8

	19 litres	23 litres	25 litres
Total liquor (litres)	26.2	31.8	34.5
Mash liquor (litres)	7.2	8.8	9.5

Mash schedule 67°C (153°F), 90 minutes

Boil time 90 minutes

Final gravity 1009

Alcohol content (ABV) 3.3%

Bitterness units (EBU) 21

Colour (EBC) 80

Malt extract version - Replace the pale malt with the appropriate quantity of pale-coloured, premium-grade malt extract and brew using the malt extract brewing method.

	19 litres	23 litres	25 litres
Malt Extract Syrup (grams)	1870	2260	2450
or			
Dried Malt Extract (grams)	1610	1940	2110

★
JENNINGS DARK MILD

A well-balanced, dark-brown Mild with a malty aroma, strong roast taste, not over-sweet, with some hops and a slightly bitter finish.

ORIGINAL GRAVITY
1031

	19 litres	23 litres	25 litres
Pale Malt (grams)	1980	2390	2600
White sugar (grams)	245	295	325
Torrefied Wheat (grams)	120	150	160
Black Malt (grams)	120	150	160
Start of Boil			
Challenger Hops (grams)	14	18	19
Fuggle Hops (grams)	8	9	10
Post-Boil Hops			
Golding Hops (grams)	5	5	6
Total liquor (litres)	25.6	31	33.6
Mash liquor (litres)	5.5	6.7	7.2

Mash schedule 67°C (153°F), 90 minutes
Boil time 90 minutes
Final gravity 1006
Alcohol content (ABV) 3.3%
Bitterness units (EBU) 22
Colour (EBC) 68

McMULLEN AK

A pleasant mix of malt and hops leads to a distinctive, dry aftertaste.
AK was originally regarded as a light Mild by McMullen.

ORIGINAL GRAVITY

1036

	19 litres	23 litres	25 litres
Pale Malt (grams)	2990	3620	3940
Chocolate Malt (grams)	43	52	56
Start of Boil			
Whitbread Golding Hops (grams)	24	29	31
Last Ten Minutes of Boil			
Whitbread Golding Hops (grams)	8	10	10
Irish Moss (grams)	3	3	3
Total liquor (litres)	26.4	32	34.7
Mash liquor (litres)	7.5	9.2	10

Mash schedule 67°C (153°F), 90 minutes
Boil time 90 minutes
Final gravity 1009
Alcohol content (ABV) 3.6%
Bitterness units (EBU) 22
Colour (EBC) 24

Malt extract version - Replace the pale malt with the appropriate quantity of pale-coloured, premium-grade malt extract and brew using the malt extract brewing method.

	19 litres	23 litres	25 litres
Malt Extract Syrup (grams)	2250	2720	2970
or			
Dried Malt Extract (grams)	1940	2340	2550

SARAH HUGHES DARK RUBY

A dark ruby strong ale, with a gravity of the Milds of yesteryear; a good balance of fruit and hops, leading to a pleasant lingering hops and malt finish.

ORIGINAL GRAVITY
1058

	19 litres	23 litres	25 litres
Pale Malt (grams)	4220	5110	5560
Crystal Malt (grams)	745	900	980
Start of Boil			
Fuggle Hops (grams)	25	31	33
Golding Hops (grams)	22	26	29
Last Ten Minutes of Boil			
Fuggle Hops (grams)	16	19	21
Total liquor (litres)	28.3	34.3	37.2
Mash liquor (litres)	12.3	15	16.3

Mash schedule 67°C (153°F), 90 minutes
Boil time 90 minutes
Final gravity 1015
Alcohol content (ABV) 5.7%
Bitterness units (EBU) 30
Colour (EBC) 47

Malt extract version - Replace the pale malt with the appropriate quantity of pale-coloured, premium-grade malt extract and brew using the malt extract brewing method.

	19 litres	23 litres	25 litres
Malt Extract Syrup (grams)	3180	3850	4190
or			
Dried Malt Extract (grams)	2730	3310	3600

THWAITES DARK MILD

A tasty traditional dark Mild presenting a malty
flavour with caramel notes and a slightly bitter finish.

ORIGINAL GRAVITY
1034

	19 litres	23 litres	25 litres
Pale Malt (grams)	2260	2730	2970
Crystal Malt (grams)	280	340	370
Black Malt (grams)	140	170	185
White Sugar (grams)	140	170	185

Start of Boil

Challenger Hops (grams)	20	24	26

Last Ten Minutes of Boil

Fuggles Hops (grams)	7	8	9
Total liquor (litres)	26	31.5	34.2
Mash liquor (litres)	6.6	8.1	8.8

Mash schedule 67°C (153°F), 90 minutes
Boil time 90 minutes
Final gravity 1008
Alcohol content (ABV) 3.4%
Bitterness units (EBU) 22
Colour (EBC) 100

Malt extract version - Replace the pale malt with the appropriate quantity of pale-
coloured, premium-grade malt extract and brew using the malt extract brewing method.

	19 litres	23 litres	25 litres
Malt Extract Syrup (grams)	1700	2050	2240
or			
Dried Malt Extract (grams)	1460	1770	1920

Pale Ale & Bitter Recipes

In the beginning, British ales were brown beers – so named because of the colour imparted to the beer by the brown malt used to make it. Milds, Porters and Stouts are direct descendants of the brown-beer tradition.

Pale ale has always been around, at least from the mid 1600s, but pale is a relative term and we really do not know how pale early pale ales were; certainly not as pale as today.

Pale ale required a pale-coloured malt, and this was quite difficult to produce with the fuels and methods of the day. Pale malt had a cleaner taste and did not have the degree of smokiness inherent in most brown malts. It required a smokeless fuel, and had to be dried at a much lower temperature over a longer period, taking an uneconomic four or five days rather than the 24 hours of brown malt. It was mostly produced by small-scale country brewers, and the resulting pale ales were expensive.

The only truly smokeless fuel available to the majority of brewers was charcoal, and though charcoal was sometimes used for pale malt, charcoal was expensive and large quantities were needed to dry moderate amounts of malt. Coal and coke were suitable alternatives, but only economical for breweries situated close to the coast or a navigable river.

The major change came with the advent of canals and later the railways which enabled large quantities of coal to be transported cheaply across country. Brewers well inland could now obtain coal. Pale malt as we know it today really stems from the late 1700s and early 1800s, and the growth of British pale ale and its breweries expanded alongside the canals and railways, and in tune with them. Access to cheap coal and coke gave the brewers access to pale malt, therefore the first breweries to specialise in pale ale were those sited beside canals. This not only gave them access to coal, but also provided them with the means of transporting their pale ale to their markets.

In the early 1800s outward-bound freight charges to India were very low as the Anglo-Indian trade was mostly homeward-bound and ships were often forced to travel to India empty. British brewers were able to take advantages of this and supply the Indian market with pale ale at a reasonable price. Where there is a British colony there is also a demand for British beer, and the East India Company themselves shipped beer to India, including pale ale, to satisfy this market.

The Burton brewers were not the sort to miss a trick. They had been exporting their brown ale to Russia for years and they wanted to cash-in on the Indian market. They made several attempts to brew pale ale, but failed and gave up the idea. In the early part of the nineteenth century, Napoleon blockaded the Baltic ports, which seriously affected the business of the Burton brewers. They were then forced to find alternative markets or die; many of them died. However, the East India Shipping Company suggested to Samuel Allsopp, a Burton brewer, that he brew a pale ale for the Indian market. Allsopp had attempted to brew pale ale before and failed, but nevertheless he had another try.

It is not clear why the Burton brewers had such difficulty in producing pale ale; it had been around for more than one hundred years by 1822. However, the first pale ale to be produced in Burton-upon-Trent was brewed in 1822 by Job Goodhead, head brewer of Allsopp's brewery – in a teapot! Bass started brewing pale ale the following year, and the Indian market was opened to the two major Burton brewers. The ale was named East India Pale Ale because it was brewed under contract to the East India Shipping Company.

From about 1830 onwards English pale ale swept across the country and then across the world. The industrialisation of Britain required plentiful supplies of coal at a reasonable price, and the extraction of coal gas provided coke as one of its by-products. All of this had the effect of lowering the cost of pale ale in comparison to the more conventional beers, and a home market for pale ale developed.

Brewing became Britain's second largest industry, second only to cotton. Although many breweries across Britain took to brewing pale ale, Bass grew to be the largest and most famous. James Herbert who referred to himself as a 'Practical Brewer of Burton-upon-Trent', stated in 1871 that the Burton brewers achieve the soft agreeable flavour to their ales by never boiling their worts hard. They used higher quantities of hops and merely simmered them for an extended period of three hours or more. However, Bass were certainly not simmering their ales by 1887, they were boiling them vigorously; although they were still boiling them for three hours.

A modern pale ale, by comparison, would be boiled vigorously for about one-and-a-half hours typically.

ADNAMS BITTER

TASTING NOTES:

Hops dominate the nose of this tawny-coloured Bitter.
Citrus hop flavours give way to a long, lingering aftertaste.

ORIGINAL GRAVITY

1036

	19 litres	23 litres	25 litres
Pale Malt (grams)	2520	3050	3320
White Sugar (grams)	280	340	370
Black Malt (grams)	40	49	53
Start of Boil			
Boadicea Hops (grams)	29	35	38
Last Ten Minutes of Boil			
Golding Hops (grams)	12	15	16
Irish Moss (grams)	3	3	3
Total liquor (litres)	25.9	31.4	34.1
Mash liquor (litres)	6.4	7.8	8.4

Mash schedule 66°C (151°F), 90 minutes

Boil time 90 minutes

Final gravity 1006

Alcohol content (ABV) 4%

Bitterness units (EBU) 33

Colour (EBC) 26

Malt extract version – Replace the pale malt with the appropriate quantity of pale-coloured, premium-grade malt extract and brew using the malt extract brewing method.

	19 litres	23 litres	25 litres
Malt Extract Syrup (grams)	1890	2290	2490
or			
Dried Malt Extract (grams)	1625	1970	2140

★
ADNAMS BROADSIDE

Grainy and dark brown; a complex, fruity beer. Rich fruity hop flavours give way to a long fruity aftertaste.

ORIGINAL GRAVITY
1045

	19 litres	23 litres	25 litres
Pale Malt (grams)	3180	3850	4180
Acid Malt (grams)	255	310	335
White Sugar (grams)	180	220	240
Black Malt (grams)	60	70	78
Start of Boil			
Challenger Hops (grams)	32	39	42
Last Ten Minutes of Boil			
Irish Moss (grams)	3	3	3
Post-boil hops			
Fuggles Hops (grams)	6	8	9
Total liquor (litres)	26.8	32.5	35.3
Mash liquor (litres)	8.7	10.6	11.5

Mash schedule 66°C (151°F), 90 minutes
Boil time 90 minutes
Final gravity 1009
Alcohol content (ABV) 4.8%
Bitterness units (EBU) 33
Colour (EBC) 37

★

ADNAMS EXPLORER

Brewed with American hops, hence the name.
Citrus fruit in the mouth, with a long sweet aftertaste.

ORIGINAL GRAVITY
1042

	19 litres	23 litres	25 litres
Pale Malt (grams)	2940	3560	3870
Crystal Malt (grams)	170	205	225
White Sugar (grams)	170	205	225
Acid Malt (grams)	135	165	180
Black Malt (grams)	28	33	36
Start of Boil			
Liberty Hops (grams)	40	48	52
Last Ten Minutes of Boil			
Irish Moss (grams)	3	3	3
Post-boil hops			
Liberty Hops (grams)	8	10	10
Total liquor (litres)	26.6	32.3	35.1
Mash liquor (litres)	8.1	9.9	10.7

Mash schedule 66°C (151°F), 90 minutes

Boil time 90 minutes

Final gravity 1009

Alcohol content (ABV) 4.4%

Bitterness units (EBU) 42

Colour (EBC) 30

Many of the Bitter and pale ale recipes, such as this one, specify small quantities of black malt as a substitute for caramel, to adjust the colour of the beer to the brewer's specified value. All brewers perform some form of colour adjustment and many of them do, in fact, use black malt extract for colour adjustment these days. However, the small quantities of black malt can be omitted from the paler beers if desired without affecting the quality of the finished beer.

PALE ALE & BITTER RECIPES

ARCHERS BEST

Bitter with a malty, fruity aroma and a pronounced bitter finish.

ORIGINAL GRAVITY
1040

	19 litres	23 litres	25 litres
Pale Malt (grams)	3220	3900	4230
Crystal Malt (grams)	165	205	220
Start of Boil			
Progress Hops (grams)	20	24	26
Whitbread Golding Hops (grams)	20	24	26
Last Ten Minutes of Boil			
Whitbread Golding Hops (grams)	13	16	17
Irish Moss (grams)	3	3	3
Total liquor (litres)	26.7	32.4	35.2
Mash liquor (litres)	8.5	10.3	11.1

Mash schedule 66°C (151°F), 90 minutes

Boil time 90 minutes

Final gravity 1010

Alcohol content (ABV) 4%

Bitterness units (EBU) 36

Colour (EBC) 15

Malt extract version – Replace the pale malt with the appropriate quantity of pale-coloured, premium-grade malt extract and brew using the malt extract brewing method.

	19 litres	23 litres	25 litres
Malt Extract Syrup (grams)	2420	2930	3170
or			
Dried Malt Extract (grams)	2080	2520	2730

★ ARCHERS VILLAGE

A dry, well-balanced beer with a full body for its gravity. Malty and fruity on the nose, then a fresh, hoppy flavour with balancing malt and a hoppy, fruity finish.

ORIGINAL GRAVITY

1035

	19 litres	23 litres	25 litres
Pale Malt (grams)	2820	3410	3700
Crystal Malt (grams)	145	175	195
Start of Boil			
Progress Hops (grams)	16	19	21
Whitbread Golding Hops (grams)	16	19	21
Last Ten Minutes of Boil			
Whitbread Golding Hops (grams)	10	13	14
Irish Moss (grams)	3	3	3
Total liquor (litres)	26.3	31.9	34.6
Mash liquor (litres)	7.4	9	9.7

Mash schedule 66°C (151°F), 90 minutes

Boil time 90 minutes

Final gravity 1008

Alcohol content (ABV) 3.6%

Bitterness units (EBU) 30

Colour (EBC) 13

· ·

Malt extract version – Replace the pale malt with the appropriate quantity of pale-coloured, premium-grade malt extract and brew using the malt extract brewing method.

	19 litres	23 litres	25 litres
Malt Extract Syrup (grams)	2120	2360	2780
or			
Dried Malt Extract (grams)	1820	2030	2390

ARKELLS 3B

A medium brown beer with a strong, sweetish malt/caramel flavour. The hops come through in the aftertaste, which is lingering and dry.

ORIGINAL GRAVITY
1040

	19 litres	23 litres	25 litres
Pale Malt (grams)	2880	3490	3790
Crystal Malt (grams)	405	490	530
White Sugar (grams)	68	82	89
Black Malt (grams)	17	20	22
Start of Boil			
Fuggle Hops (grams)	22	26	29
Golding Hops (grams)	19	23	25
Last Ten Minutes of Boil			
Golding Hops (grams)	13	16	18
Irish Moss (grams)	3	3	3
Total liquor (litres)	26.6	32.3	35.1
Mash liquor (litres)	8.2	10	10.8

Mash schedule 66°C (151°F), 90 minutes
Boil time 90 minutes
Final gravity 1009
Alcohol content (ABV) 4.1%
Bitterness units (EBU) 30
Colour (EBC) 35

Malt extract version – Replace the pale malt with the appropriate quantity of pale-coloured, premium-grade malt extract and brew using the malt extract brewing method.

	19 litres	23 litres	25 litres
Malt Extract Syrup (grams)	2160	2612	2840
or			
Dried Malt Extract (grams)	1860	2250	2450

ARKELLS KINGSDOWN ALE

A stronger version of 3B. A rich, deep, russet-coloured beer.
The malty/fruity aroma continues in the taste which has a hint of pears.
The hops come through in the aftertaste where they
are complemented by caramel tones.

ORIGINAL GRAVITY
1052

	19 litres	23 litres	25 litres
Pale Malt (grams)	3750	4540	4940
Crystal Malt (grams)	525	635	690
White Sugar (grams)	88	105	115
Black Malt (grams)	18	21	23
Start of Boil			
Fuggle Hops (grams)	26	31	34
Golding Hops (grams)	22	27	29
Last Ten Minutes of Boil			
Golding Hops (grams)	16	19	21
Irish Moss (grams)	3	3	3
Total liquor (litres)	27.6	33.5	36.4
Mash liquor (litres)	10.7	13	14.1

Mash schedule 66°C (151°F), 90 minutes
Boil time 90 minutes
Final gravity 1012
Alcohol content (ABV) 5.3%
Bitterness units (EBU) 32
Colour (EBC) 43

Malt extract version – Replace the pale malt with the appropriate quantity of pale-coloured, premium-grade malt extract and brew using the malt extract brewing method.

	19 litres	23 litres	25 litres
Malt Extract Syrup (grams)	2810	3410	3710
or			
Dried Malt Extract (grams)	2420	2930	3190

BANKS'S BITTER

A pale brown Bitter with a pleasant balance of hops and malt. Hops continue from the taste through to a bitter-sweet aftertaste.

ORIGINAL GRAVITY
1038

	19 litres	**23 litres**	**25 litres**
Pale Malt (grams)	3170	3840	4170
Black Malt (grams)	32	39	42
Start of Boil			
Fuggle Hops (grams)	47	57	62
Last Ten Minutes of Boil			
Golding Hops (grams)	16	19	21
Irish Moss (grams)	3	3	3
Total liquor (litres)	26.6	32.2	35
Mash liquor (litres)	8	9.7	10.5

Mash schedule 66°C (151°F), 90 minutes
Boil time 90 minutes
Final gravity 1009
Alcohol content (ABV) 3.8%
Bitterness units (EBU) 33
Colour (EBC) 23

Malt extract version – Replace the pale malt with the appropriate quantity of pale-coloured, premium-grade malt extract and brew using the malt extract brewing method.

	19 litres	**23 litres**	**25 litres**
Malt Extract Syrup (grams)	2380	2880	3130
or			
Dried Malt Extract (grams)	2050	2480	2690

★
BANKS'S ORIGINAL

An amber-coloured, well balanced, refreshing session beer.

ORIGINAL GRAVITY
1036

	19 litres	23 litres	25 litres
Pale Malt (grams)	2970	3600	3910
Black Malt (grams)	67	81	88
Start of Boil			
Fuggle Hops (grams)	36	43	47
Last Ten Minutes of Boil			
Golding Hops (grams)	12	14	15
Irish Moss (grams)	3	3	3
Total liquor (litres)	26.4	32	34.7
Mash liquor (litres)	7.5	9.2	10

Mash schedule 66°C (151°F), 90 minutes

Boil time 90 minutes

Final gravity 1009

Alcohol content (ABV) 3.6%

Bitterness units (EBU) 25

Colour (EBC) 40

Malt extract version – Replace the pale malt with the appropriate quantity of pale-coloured, premium-grade malt extract and brew using the malt extract brewing method.

	19 litres	23 litres	25 litres
Malt Extract Syrup (grams)	2230	2700	2930
or			
Dried Malt Extract (grams)	1920	2320	2520

BASS DRAUGHT BASS

Pale brown with a fruity aroma and a hint of hops. Hoppy
but sweet taste with malt, then a lingering hoppy bitterness.
Until rcently Britain's most widely-sold beer. Now brewed in compara-
tively small volumes by Marstons under contract for InBev UK.

ORIGINAL GRAVITY

1043

	19 litres	23 litres	25 litres
Pale Malt (grams)	3460	4190	4550
Crystal Malt (grams)	180	220	240
Start of Boil			
Challenger Hops (grams)	25	30	33
Last Ten Minutes of Boil			
Irish Moss (grams)	3	3	3
Total liquor (litres)	27	32.7	35.5
Mash liquor (litres)	9	11	11.9

Mash schedule 66°C (151°F), 90 minutes
Boil time 90 minutes
Final gravity 1010
Alcohol content (ABV) 4.4%
Bitterness units (EBU) 26
Colour (EBC) 16

Malt extract version – Replace the pale malt with the appropriate quantity of pale-
coloured, premium-grade malt extract and brew using the malt extract brewing method.

	19 litres	23 litres	25 litres
Malt Extract Syrup (grams)	2600	3140	3410
or			
Dried Malt Extract (grams)	2230	2700	2940

★
BATEMANS VICTORY ALE

Luscious aromas of hops, oranges and pear drops. Full malt in the mouth, intense finish with complex balance of hop bitterness and fruit.

ORIGINAL GRAVITY
1054

	19 litres	23 litres	25 litres
Pale Malt (grams)	3860	4670	5070
White Sugar (grams)	345	420	455
Crystal Malt (grams)	130	155	170
Start of Boil			
Golding Hops (grams)	25	30	33
Styrian Golding Hops (grams)	25	30	33
Last Ten Minutes of Boil			
Styrian Golding Hops (grams)	16	20	22
Irish Moss (grams)	3	3	3
Total liquor (litres)	27.3	33.1	35.9
Mash liquor (litres)	9.9	12.1	13.1

Mash schedule 66°C (151°F), 90 minutes
Boil time 90 minutes
Final gravity 1010
Alcohol content (ABV) 5.8%
Bitterness units (EBU) 32
Colour (EBC) 14

Malt extract version – Replace the pale malt with the appropriate quantity of pale-coloured, premium-grade malt extract and brew using the malt extract brewing method.

	19 litres	23 litres	25 litres
Malt Extract Syrup (grams)	2900	3500	3800
or			
Dried Malt Extract (grams)	2490	3010	3270

BATEMANS XXXB

A brilliant blend of malt, hops and fruit on the nose with a bitter bite over the top of a faintly banana maltiness that stays the course. A russet-tan brown classic.

ORIGINAL GRAVITY
1049

	19 litres	23 litres	25 litres
Pale Malt (grams)	2790	3380	3670
Crystal Malt (grams)	455	555	600
White Sugar (grams)	545	660	715
Black Malt (grams)	27	32	35

Start of Boil

Challenger Hops (grams)	37	45	49

Last Ten Minutes of Boil

Irish Moss (grams)	3	3	3
Total liquor (litres)	26.6	32.3	35.1
Mash liquor (litres)	8.1	9.9	10.7

Mash schedule 66°C (151°F), 90 minutes
Boil time 90 minutes
Final gravity 1007
Alcohol content (ABV) 5.6%
Bitterness units (EBU) 37
Colour (EBC) 43

Malt extract version – Replace the pale malt with the appropriate quantity of pale-coloured, premium-grade malt extract and brew using the malt extract brewing method.

	19 litres	23 litres	25 litres
Malt Extract Syrup (grams)	2090	2540	2750
or			
Dried Malt Extract (grams)	1800	2180	2370

BATHAMS BEST BITTER

A pale yellow, fruity, sweetish Bitter with a dry, hoppy finish. A good, light, refreshing beer.

ORIGINAL GRAVITY
1044

	19 litres	23 litres	25 litres
Pale Malt (grams)	3700	4480	4870
Start of Boil			
Fuggle Hops (grams)	22	27	30
Northdown Hops (grams)	13	16	17
Last Ten Minutes of Boil			
Irish Moss (grams)	3	3	3
Post-boil Hops			
Golding Hops (grams)	7	9	9
Total liquor (litres)	27	32.8	35.6
Mash liquor (litres)	9.2	11.2	12.1

Mash schedule 66°C (151°F), 90 minutes
Boil time 90 minutes
Final gravity 1010
Alcohol content (ABV) 4.5%
Bitterness units (EBU) 30
Colour (EBC) 7

Malt extract version – Replace the pale malt with the appropriate quantity of pale-coloured, premium-grade malt extract and brew using the malt extract brewing method.

	19 litres	23 litres	25 litres
Malt Extract Syrup (grams)	2780	3360	3650
or			
Dried Malt Extract (grams)	2390	2890	3140

BELHAVEN 80/-

One of the few remaining Scottish eighty-shillings, with malt the predominant flavour characteristic, though it is balanced by hop and fruit. Roast and caramel malts play a part in this complex beer.

ORIGINAL GRAVITY

1040

	19 litres	23 litres	25 litres
Pale Malt (grams)	2850	3450	3750
White Sugar (grams)	245	295	320
Crystal Malt (grams)	81	98	105
Black Malt (grams)	48	59	64

Start of Boil

Whitbread Golding Hops (grams)	32	39	42

Last Ten Minutes of Boil

Whitbread Golding Hops (grams)	11	13	14
Irish Moss (grams)	3	3	3

Total liquor (litres)	26.3	31.9	34.6
Mash liquor (litres)	7.4	9	9.7

Mash schedule 66°C (151°F), 90 minutes

Boil time 90 minutes

Final gravity 1008

Alcohol content (ABV) 4.2%

Bitterness units (EBU) 29

Colour (EBC) 35

Malt extract version – Replace the pale malt with the appropriate quantity of pale-coloured, premium-grade malt extract and brew using the malt extract brewing method.

	19 litres	23 litres	25 litres
Malt Extract Syrup (grams)	2140	2587	2821
or			
Dried Malt Extract (grams)	1840	2230	2420

BELHAVEN 90/-

A great beer with a distinctive hop aroma and palate. Rich and peppery hop aroma with fruit notes. Full malt in the mouth; bitter-sweet finish with good hop character.

ORIGINAL GRAVITY
1070

	19 litres	23 litres	25 litres
Pale Malt (grams)	5030	6090	6620
White Sugar (grams)	445	540	590
Black Malt (grams)	125	155	170

Start of Boil

Whitbread Golding Hops (grams)	52	63	69

Last Ten Minutes of Boil

Whitbread Golding Hops (grams)	17	21	23
Irish Moss (grams)	3	3	3

Total liquor (litres)	28.5	34.6	37.6
Mash liquor (litres)	12.8	15.6	16.9

Mash schedule 66°C (151°F), 90 minutes
Boil time 90 minutes
Final gravity 1013
Alcohol content (ABV) 7.6%
Bitterness units (EBU) 36
Colour (EBC) 76

Malt extract version – Replace the pale malt with the appropriate quantity of pale-coloured, premium-grade malt extract and brew using the malt extract brewing method.

	19 litres	23 litres	25 litres
Malt Extract Syrup (grams)	3770	4570	4970
or			
Dried Malt Extract (grams)	3240	3930	4270

BIG LAMP BITTER

A clean-tasting tawny Bitter, full of hops and malt.
A hint of fruit with a good hoppy finish.

ORIGINAL GRAVITY

1040

	19 litres	23 litres	25 litres
Pale Malt (grams)	3220	3900	4230
Crystal Malt (grams)	165	205	220
Start of Boil			
Golding Hops (grams)	37	45	49
Post-boil Hops			
Fuggle Hops (grams)	7	9	10
Total liquor (litres)	26.7	32.4	35.2
Mash liquor (litres)	8.5	10.3	11.1

Mash schedule 66°C (151°F), 90 minutes

Boil time 90 minutes

Final gravity 1010

Alcohol content (ABV) 4%

Bitterness units (EBU) 30

Colour (EBC) 15

Malt extract version – Replace the pale malt with the appropriate quantity of pale-coloured, premium-grade malt extract and brew using the malt extract brewing method.

	19 litres	23 litres	25 litres
Malt Extract Syrup (grams)	2415	2930	3170
or			
Dried Malt Extract (grams)	2080	2520	2730

★
BLACK SHEEP ALE

Superb premium Bitter with robust malt, fruit and hops. Malt,
hop, cobnut and orange fruit aromas. Bitter-sweet in mouth
with dry finish packed with fruit and Goldings hops.

ORIGINAL GRAVITY
1046

	19 litres	23 litres	25 litres
Pale Malt (grams)	3260	3950	4290
Torrified Wheat (grams)	390	475	515
Crystal Malt (grams)	275	330	360
Black Malt (grams)	12	14	16
Start of Boil			
Challenger Hops (grams)	17	20	22
Progress Hops (grams)	17	20	22
Fuggle Hops (grams)	8	10	11
Last Ten Minutes of Boil			
Golding Hops (grams)	14	17	18
Irish Moss (grams)	3	3	3
Total liquor (litres)	27.3	33.1	35.9
Mash liquor (litres)	9.8	11.9	12.9

Mash schedule 66°C (151°F), 90 minutes
Boil time 90 minutes
Final gravity 1011
Alcohol content (ABV) 4.6%
Bitterness units (EBU) 36
Colour (EBC) 27

PALE ALE & BITTER RECIPES

BLACK SHEEP BEST BITTER

Pale gold ale with distinctive hop character.
Powerful attack of Fuggles with malt background.
Peppery hop in mouth and in long, bitter finish.

ORIGINAL GRAVITY
1038

	19 litres	23 litres	25 litres
Pale Malt (grams)	2760	3340	3630
Torrefied Wheat (grams)	325	390	425
Crystal Malt (grams)	160	195	210
Black Malt (grams)	7	8	9

Start of Boil

	19 litres	23 litres	25 litres
Challenger Hops (grams)	17	20	22
Fuggle Hops (grams)	8	10	11
Golding Hops (grams)	8	10	11

Last Ten Minutes of Boil

	19 litres	23 litres	25 litres
Fuggle Hops (grams)	11	13	14
Irish Moss (grams)	3	3	3

	19 litres	23 litres	25 litres
Total liquor (litres)	26.6	32.2	35
Mash liquor (litres)	8	9.8	10.6

Mash schedule 66°C (151°F), 90 minutes

Boil time 90 minutes

Final gravity 1009

Alcohol content (ABV) 3.8%

Bitterness units (EBU) 31

Colour (EBC) 18

BLACK SHEEP RIGGWELTER

Roasted malt, hops and banana fruit aromas.
Dry palate with complex mixture of hops, fruit and
roasted barley. Dry refreshing finish.

ORIGINAL GRAVITY
1056

	19 litres	23 litres	25 litres
Pale Malt (grams)	3490	4220	4590
Torrefied Wheat (grams)	410	495	540
White Sugar (grams)	320	385	420
Crystal Malt (grams)	275	330	360
Chocolate Malt (grams)	87	105	115
Start of Boil			
Challenger Hops (grams)	19	23	25
Progress Hops (grams)	19	23	25
Fuggle Hops (grams)	10	12	13
Last Ten Minutes of Boil			
Golding Hops (grams)	16	19	21
Irish Moss (grams)	3	3	3
Total liquor (litres)	27.6	33.5	36.4
Mash liquor (litres)	10.6	12.9	14

Mash schedule 66°C (151°F), 90 minutes
Boil time 90 minutes
Final gravity 1011
Alcohol content (ABV) 6%
Bitterness units (EBU) 39
Colour (EBC) 58

BODDINGTONS BITTER

A remarkable, light, golden Bitter. A fine quenching session beer. Flinty dryness in the mouth, long hard finish with hop bitterness and tart fruit. Currently brewed by Hydes in Manchester now that the Boddington's Strangeways Brewery has closed. At least prisoners at Strangeways are no longer tortured by the smell from the brewery next door.

ORIGINAL GRAVITY
1035

	19 litres	23 litres	25 litres
Pale Malt (grams)	2660	3220	3500
Crystal Malt (grams)	165	200	220
White Sugar (grams)	84	100	110

Start of Boil

Whitbread Golding Hops (grams)	32	39	42

Last Ten Minutes of Boil

Fuggle Hops (grams)	11	13	14
Irish Moss (grams)	3	3	3

Total liquor (litres)	26.1	31.7	34.4
Mash liquor (litres)	7.1	8.6	9.3

Mash schedule 66°C (151°F), 90 minutes
Boil time 90 minutes
Final gravity 1008
Alcohol content (ABV) 3.6%
Bitterness units (EBU) 30
Colour (EBC) 14

Malt extract version – Replace the pale malt with the appropriate quantity of pale-coloured, premium-grade malt extract and brew using the malt extract brewing method.

	19 litres	23 litres	25 litres
Malt Extract Syrup (grams)	1200	2420	2630
or			
Dried Malt Extract (grams)	1720	2080	2260

BRAKSPEAR BITTER

A classic copper-coloured pale ale with a big hop resins, juicy malt and orange aroma. Intense hop bitterness in the mouth and finish, and a firm maltiness and tangy fruitiness throughout.

ORIGINAL GRAVITY
1035

	19 litres	23 litres	25 litres
Pale Malt (grams)	2470	2990	3250
White Sugar (grams)	225	270	295
Crystal Malt (grams)	84	100	110
Black Malt (grams)	28	34	37
Start of Boil			
Challenger Hops (grams)	34	41	45
Last Ten Minutes of Boil			
Irish Moss (grams)	3	3	3
Post-boil Hops			
Styrian Golding Hops	7	8	9
Total liquor (litres)	25.9	31.4	34.1
Mash liquor (litres)	6.4	7.8	8.4

Mash schedule 66°C (151°F), 90 minutes
Boil time 90 minutes
Final gravity 1006
Alcohol content (ABV) 3.8%
Bitterness units (EBU) 38
Colour (EBC) 24

 Dry hop with a few cones of Golding.

Malt extract version – Replace the pale malt with the appropriate quantity of pale-coloured, premium-grade malt extract and brew using the malt extract brewing method.

	19 litres	23 litres	25 litres
Malt Extract Syrup (grams)	1850	2240	2440
or			
Dried Malt Extract (grams)	1590	1930	2100

BRAKSPEAR SPECIAL

A stronger version of their Bitter. Rich malt, hops and fruit aroma; biscuity hop and fruit resins in the mouth; long bitter-sweet finish with orange fruit notes.

ORIGINAL GRAVITY
1045

	19 litres	23 litres	25 litres
Pale Malt (grams)	3190	3860	4190
White Sugar (grams)	285	350	380
Crystal Malt (grams)	105	130	140
Black Malt (grams)	29	35	38
Start of Boil			
Challenger Hops (grams)	45	54	59
Last Ten Minutes of Boil			
Irish Moss (grams)	3	3	3
Post-boil Hops			
Styrian Golding Hops (grams)	9	11	12
Total liquor (litres)	26.6	32.3	35.1
Mash liquor (litres)	8.3	10.1	10.9

Mash schedule 66°C (151°F), 90 minutes
Boil time 90 minutes
Final gravity 1008
Alcohol content (ABV) 4.9%
Bitterness units (EBU) 46
Colour (EBC) 27

 Dry hop with a few cones of Golding.

Malt extract version – Replace the pale malt with the appropriate quantity of pale-coloured, premium-grade malt extract and brew using the malt extract brewing method.

	19 litres	23 litres	25 litres
Malt Extract Syrup (grams)	2390	2900	3140
or			
Dried Malt Extract (grams)	2060	2490	2700

BURTON BRIDGE BRIDGE BITTER

Pale brown and hoppy with a hint of roast and caramel.
Complex taste with hops just dominating to
provide a lingering hoppy finish.

ORIGINAL GRAVITY
1041

	19 litres	23 litres	25 litres
Pale Malt (grams)	3080	3730	4050
Crystal Malt (grams)	165	205	220
White Sugar (grams)	135	160	175
Start of Boil			
Challenger Hops (grams)	17	20	22
Target Hops (grams)	11	13	15
Last Ten Minutes of Boil			
Irish Moss (grams)	3	3	3
Post-boil Hops (grams)			
Styrian Golding Hops (grams	6	7	7
Total liquor (litres)	26.6	32.2	35
Mash liquor (litres)	8	9.8	10.6

Mash schedule 66°C (151°F), 90 minutes
Boil time 90 minutes
Final gravity 1009
Alcohol content (ABV) 4.2%
Bitterness units (EBU) 35
Colour (EBC) 15

Malt extract version – Replace the pale malt with the appropriate quantity of pale-coloured, premium-grade malt extract and brew using the malt extract brewing method.

	19 litres	23 litres	25 litres
Malt Extract Syrup (grams)	2310	2780	3040
or			
Dried Malt Extract (grams)	1990	2410	2610

BURTON BRIDGE GOLDEN DELICIOUS

Golden as named, fruity as intended and tasty as anticipated.
This beer is a Burton classic with sulphurous aroma, well-balanced hops and fruit, and a mouth-watering bitter finish.

ORIGINAL GRAVITY

1038

	19 litres	23 litres	25 litres
Pale Malt (grams)	2990	3620	3940
White Sugar (grams)	125	150	160

Start of Boil

	19 litres	23 litres	25 litres
Challenger Hops (grams)	22	26	28

Last Ten Minutes of Boil

	19 litres	23 litres	25 litres
Styrian Golding Hops (grams	7	9	9
Irish Moss (grams)	3	3	3
Total liquor (litres)	26.3	31.9	34.6
Mash liquor (litres)	7.5	9.1	9.8

Mash schedule 66°C (151°F), 90 minutes
Boil time 90 minutes
Final gravity 1008
Alcohol content (ABV) 4%
Bitterness units (EBU) 30
Colour (EBC) 6

· ·

Malt extract version – Replace the pale malt with the appropriate quantity of pale-coloured, premium-grade malt extract and brew using the malt extract brewing method.

	19 litres	23 litres	25 litres
Malt Extract Syrup (grams)	2240	2720	2960
or			
Dried Malt Extract (grams)	1930	2335	2540

BURTON BRIDGE XL BITTER

A golden malty Bitter with fruit and hoppy aromas.
Hoppy and bitter finish with a characteristic astringent aftertaste.

ORIGINAL GRAVITY
1039

	19 litres	23 litres	25 litres
Pale Malt (grams)	3230	3900	4240
Chocolate Malt (grams)	66	80	87
Start of Boil			
Challenger Hops (grams)	12	14	15
Target Hops (grams)	12	14	15
Last Ten Minutes of Boil			
Target Hops (grams)	8	9	10
Irish Moss (grams)	3	3	3
Total liquor (litres)	26.6	32.2	35.1
Mash liquor (litres)	8.2	10	10.8

Mash schedule 66°C (151°F), 90 minutes
Boil time 90 minutes
Final gravity 1009
Alcohol content (ABV) 4%
Bitterness units (EBU) 30
Colour (EBC) 34

Malt extract version – Replace the pale malt with the appropriate quantity of pale-coloured, premium-grade malt extract and brew using the malt extract brewing method.

	19 litres	23 litres	25 litres
Malt Extract Syrup (grams)	2420	2930	3180
or			
Dried Malt Extract (grams)	2080	2520	2740

CALEDONIAN 80/-

A predominantly malty, copper-coloured beer with underlying fruit. A Scottish heavy that now lacks the complex taste and hoppiness of old. The name refers to eighty-shillings. Sometimes called slash-dash, presumably by those who were born after 1971 and have no idea what a shilling was.

ORIGINAL GRAVITY
1042

	19 litres	23 litres	25 litres
Pale Malt (grams)	3250	3930	4270
Crystal Malt (grams)	175	215	230
Wheat Malt (grams)	105	125	140
Chocolate Malt (grams)	25	30	33
Start of Boil			
Fuggle Hops (grams)	26	31	34
Golding Hops (grams)	22	27	29
Last Ten Minutes of Boil			
Golding Hops (grams)	16	19	21
Irish Moss (grams)	3	3	3
Total liquor (litres)	26.9	32.6	35.4
Mash liquor (litres)	8.9	10.8	11.7

Mash schedule 66°C (151°F), 90 minutes

Boil time 90 minutes

Final gravity 1010

Alcohol content (ABV) 4.2%

Bitterness units (EBU) 35

Colour (EBC) 26

★
CALEDONIAN DEUCHARS IPA

At its best, an extremely tasty and refreshing, amber-
coloured session beer. Hops and fruit are evident and are
balanced by malt throughout. The lingering aftertaste is delightfully bitter and hoppy.

ORIGINAL GRAVITY
1038

	19 litres	23 litres	25 litres
Pale Malt (grams)	2930	3550	3860
Crystal Malt (grams)	190	230	250
Wheat Malt (grams)	97	115	125
Start of Boil			
Fuggle Hops (grams)	50	61	66
Last Ten Minutes of Boil			
Styrian Golding Hops (grams)	17	20	22
Irish Moss (grams)	3	3	3
Total liquor (litres)	26.6	32.2	35
Mash liquor (litres)	8	9.8	10.6

Mash schedule 66°C (151°F), 90 minutes
Boil time 90 minutes
Final gravity 1009
Alcohol content (ABV) 3.8%
Bitterness units (EBU) 35
Colour (EBC) 16

CAMERONS BEST BITTER

A light Bitter, but well balanced with hops and malt. Seems to have been renamed Best Bitter in recent months; hardly 'best' at 3.6%, but there we go.

ORIGINAL GRAVITY

1036

	19 litres	23 litres	25 litres
Pale Malt (grams)	2870	3480	3780
Crystal Malt (grams)	150	185	200
Black Malt (grams)	24	30	32
Start of Boil			
Target Hops (grams)	18	22	24
Last Ten Minutes of Boil			
Styrian Golding Hops (grams)	6	7	8
Irish Moss (grams)	3	3	3
Total liquor (litres)	26.4	32	34.7
Mash liquor (litres)	7.5	9.2	10

Mash schedule 66°C (151°F), 90 minutes

Boil time 90 minutes

Final gravity 1009

Alcohol content (ABV) 3.6%

Bitterness units (EBU) 30

Colour (EBC) 26

Malt extract version – Replace the pale malt with the appropriate quantity of pale-coloured, premium-grade malt extract and brew using the malt extract brewing method.

	19 litres	23 litres	25 litres
Malt Extract Syrup (grams)	2150	2610	2840
or			
Dried Malt Extract (grams)	1859	2250	2440

CAMERONS CASTLE EDEN ALE

A light, creamy, malty, sweet ale with fruit notes and
a mellow dry bitterness in the finish.

ORIGINAL GRAVITY
1040

	19 litres	23 litres	25 litres
Pale Malt (grams)	2800	3380	3680
Torrefied Wheat (grams)	325	395	430
White Sugar (grams)	160	195	215
Start of Boil			
Target Hops (grams)	17	21	23
Last Ten Minutes of Boil			
Styrian Golding Hops (grams)	6	7	8
Irish Moss (grams)	3	3	3
Total liquor (litres)	26.5	32.1	34.8
Mash liquor (litres)	7.8	9.5	10.3

Mash schedule 66°C (151°F), 90 minutes

Boil time 90 minutes

Final gravity 1008

Alcohol content (ABV) 4.2%

Bitterness units (EBU) 28

Colour (EBC) 6

CAMERONS STRONGARM

A well-rounded ruby-red ale with a distinctive, light creamy head; initially fruity but with a good balance of malt, hops and moderate bitterness.

ORIGINAL GRAVITY
1040

	19 litres	23 litres	25 litres
Pale Malt (grams)	2620	3180	3450
White Sugar (grams)	315	385	415
Crystal Malt (grams)	155	190	210
Black Malt (grams)	83	100	105

Start of Boil

	19 litres	23 litres	25 litres
Challenger Hops (grams)	28	34	37

Last Ten Minutes of Boil

	19 litres	23 litres	25 litres
Golding Hops (grams)	9	11	12
Irish Moss (grams)	3	3	3

	19 litres	23 litres	25 litres
Total liquor (litres)	26.2	31.8	34.5
Mash liquor (litres)	7.1	8.7	9.4

Mash schedule 66°C (151°F), 90 minutes
Boil time 90 minutes
Final gravity 1007
Alcohol content (ABV) 4.4%
Bitterness units (EBU) 30
Colour (EBC) 56

Malt extract version – Replace the pale malt with the appropriate quantity of pale-coloured, premium-grade malt extract and brew using the malt extract brewing method.

	19 litres	23 litres	25 litres
Malt Extract Syrup (grams)	1970	2390	2590
or			
Dried Malt Extract (grams)	1690	2050	2230

★
COTLEIGH BARN OWL

A pale to mid-brown beer with a good balance of malt and hops on the nose; a smooth, full-bodied taste where hops dominate, but balanced by malt following through to the finish.

ORIGINAL GRAVITY
1045

	19 litres	23 litres	25 litres
Pale Malt (grams)	3550	4300	4670
Crystal Malt (grams)	190	230	250
Chocolate Malt (grams)	76	93	100
Start of Boil			
Northdown Hops (grams)	29	35	38
Last Ten Minutes of Boil			
Irish Moss (grams)	3	3	3
Post-boil Hops			
Fuggle Hops (grams)	6	7	8
Total liquor (litres)	27.1	32.9	35.7
Mash liquor (litres)	9.5	11.6	12.6

Mash schedule 66°C (151°F), 90 minutes
Boil time 90 minutes
Final gravity 1011
Alcohol content (ABV) 4.5%
Bitterness units (EBU) 32
Colour (EBC) 49

Malt extract version – Replace the pale malt with the appropriate quantity of pale-coloured, premium-grade malt extract and brew using the malt extract brewing method.

	19 litres	23 litres	25 litres
Malt Extract Syrup (grams)	2660	3230	3500
or			
Dried Malt Extract (grams)	2290	2770	3010

COTLEIGH TAWNEY BITTER

Well-balanced, tawny-coloured Bitter with plenty of malt and fruitiness on the nose, and malt to the fore in the taste, followed by hop fruit, developing into a satisfying bitter finish.

ORIGINAL GRAVITY
1038

	19 litres	23 litres	25 litres
Pale Malt (grams)	2970	3600	3910
Crystal Malt (grams)	255	310	340
Start of Boil			
Challenger Hops (grams)	16	19	21
Fuggle Hops (grams)	16	19	21
Last Ten Minutes of Boil			
Irish Moss (grams)	3	3	3
Post-boil Hops			
Golding Hops (grams)	6	8	8
Total liquor (litres)	26.6	32.2	35
Mash liquor (litres)	8	9.8	10.6

Mash schedule 66°C (151°F), 90 minutes

Boil time 90 minutes

Final gravity 1009

Alcohol content (ABV) 3.8%

Bitterness units (EBU) 28

Colour (EBC) 19

Malt extract version – Replace the pale malt with the appropriate quantity of pale-coloured, premium-grade malt extract and brew using the malt extract brewing method.

	19 litres	23 litres	25 litres
Malt Extract Syrup (grams)	2230	2700	2930
or			
Dried Malt Extract (grams)	1920	2320	2520

COURAGE BEST BITTER

A ruby coloured, malt accented Bitter from
Courage's Bristol brewery. Malt and toffee notes in
the mouth, dry finish with hop character.

ORIGINAL GRAVITY

1039

	19 litres	23 litres	25 litres
Pale Malt (grams)	2680	3250	3530
White Sugar (grams)	250	300	330
Crystal Malt (grams)	185	225	245
Black Malt (grams)	19	23	25
Start of Boil			
Target Hops (grams)	17	20	22
Last Ten Minutes of Boil			
Irish Moss (grams)	3	3	3
Post-boil Hops			
Styrian Golding Hops (grams)	3	4	4
Total liquor (litres)	26.2	31.8	34.5
Mash liquor (litres)	7.2	8.8	9.5

Mash schedule 66°C (151°F), 90 minutes

Boil time 90 minutes

Final gravity 1007

Alcohol content (ABV) 4.2%

Bitterness units (EBU) 27

Colour (EBC) 25

Malt extract version – Replace the pale malt with the appropriate quantity of pale-coloured, premium-grade malt extract and brew using the malt extract brewing method.

	19 litres	23 litres	25 litres
Malt Extract Syrup (grams)	2010	2440	2650
or			
Dried Malt Extract (grams)	1730	2010	2230

COURAGE DIRECTORS

A superb, full-drinking and intriguingly complex ale, excellent with traditional English dishes. Brewed at Courage's Bristol brewery. Rich and fruity in the mouth, intense bitter-sweet finish.

ORIGINAL GRAVITY
1046

	19 litres	23 litres	25 litres
Pale Malt (grams)	3160	3830	4160
White Sugar (grams)	295	355	390
Crystal Malt (grams)	220	265	290
Black Malt (grams)	22	27	29

Start of Boil

Target Hops (grams)	22	26	28

Last Ten Minutes of Boil

Irish Moss (grams)	3	3	3

Post-boil Hops

Styrian Golding Hops (grams)	4	5	6

Total liquor (litres)	26.7	32.4	35.2
Mash liquor (litres)	8.5	10.3	11.1

Mash schedule 66°C (151°F), 90 minutes

Boil time 90 minutes

Final gravity 1008

Alcohol content (ABV) 5%

Bitterness units (EBU) 33

Colour (EBC) 29

Malt extract version – Replace the pale malt with the appropriate quantity of pale-coloured, premium-grade malt extract and brew using the malt extract brewing method.

	19 litres	23 litres	25 litres
Malt Extract Syrup (grams)	2370	2870	3120
or			
Dried Malt Extract (grams)	2040	2470	2680

DONNINGTON BB

A pleasant amber Bitter with a slight hop aroma, good
balance of malt and hops in the mouth and a bitter aftertaste.

ORIGINAL GRAVITY
1035

	19 litres	23 litres	25 litres
Pale Malt (grams)	2400	2900	3150
White Sugar (grams)	225	270	295
Crystal Malt (grams)	195	235	260
Start of Boil			
Fuggle Hops (grams)	39	47	51
Last Ten Minutes of Boil			
Irish Moss (grams)	3	3	3
Total liquor (litres)	25.9	31.4	34.1
Mash liquor (litres)	6.5	7.9	8.5

Mash schedule 66°C (151°F), 90 minutes
Boil time 90 minutes
Final gravity 1006
Alcohol content (ABV) 3.8%
Bitterness units (EBU) 28
Colour (EBC) 15

Malt extract version – Replace the pale malt with the appropriate quantity of pale-
coloured, premium-grade malt extract and brew using the malt extract brewing method.

	19 litres	23 litres	25 litres
Malt Extract Syrup (grams)	1800	2180	2360
or			
Dried Malt Extract (grams)	1550	1870	2030

DONNINGTON SBA

Malt dominates over bitterness in the subtle flavour of this premium Bitter, which has a hint of fruit and a dry malty finish.

ORIGINAL GRAVITY

1040

	19 litres	23 litres	25 litres
Pale Malt (grams)	2740	3320	3610
White Sugar (grams)	255	310	335
Crystal Malt (grams)	225	270	295
Start of Boil			
Fuggle Hops (grams)	46	56	61
Last Ten Minutes of Boil			
Irish Moss (grams)	3	3	3
Total liquor (litres)	26.3	31.9	34.6
Mash liquor (litres)	7.4	9	9.7

Mash schedule 66°C (151°F), 90 minutes
Boil time 90 minutes
Final gravity 1007
Alcohol content (ABV) 4.4%
Bitterness units (EBU) 32
Colour (EBC) 17

Malt extract version – Replace the pale malt with the appropriate quantity of pale-coloured, premium-grade malt extract and brew using the malt extract brewing method.

	19 litres	23 litres	25 litres
Malt Extract Syrup (grams)	2060	2490	2710
or			
Dried Malt Extract (grams)	1770	2140	2330

EVERARDS BEACON

Light, refreshing, well-balanced pale amber
Bitter in the Burton style.

ORIGINAL GRAVITY
1036

	19 litres	23 litres	25 litres
Pale Malt (grams)	2450	2960	3220
Crystal Malt (grams)	295	355	385
White Sugar (grams)	145	175	190
Torrefied Wheat (grams)	88	105	115
Start of Boil			
Challenger Hops (grams)	22	27	29
Last Ten Minutes of Boil			
Fuggle Hops (grams)	7	9	10
Irish Moss (grams)	3	3	3
Total liquor (litres)	26.1	31.7	34.4
Mash liquor (litres)	7.1	8.6	9.3

Mash schedule 66°C (151°F), 90 minutes

Boil time 90 minutes

Final gravity 1007

Alcohol content (ABV) 3.8%

Bitterness units (EBU) 25

Colour (EBC) 20

 Dry hop with a few cones of Golding.

EVERARDS ORIGINAL

Full bodied, mid-brown strong Bitter with a pleasant rich, grainy mouthfeel. Well balanced flavours, with malt slightly to the fore, merging into a long satisfying finish.

ORIGINAL GRAVITY
1050

	19 litres	23 litres	25 litres
Pale Malt (grams)	3430	4150	4510
Crystal Malt (grams)	355	430	465
White Sugar (grams)	205	250	270
Torrefied Wheat (grams)	120	150	160
Black Malt (grams)	12	15	16
Start of Boil			
Challenger Hops (grams)	30	36	39
Last Ten Minutes of Boil			
Fuggle Hops (grams)	10	12	13
Irish Moss (grams)	3	3	3
Total liquor (litres)	27.3	33.1	35.9
Mash liquor (litres)	9.8	11.9	12.9

Mash schedule 66°C (151°F), 90 minutes

Boil time 90 minutes

Final gravity 1010

Alcohol content (ABV) 5.3%

Bitterness units (EBU) 29

Colour (EBC) 32

 Dry hop with a few cones of Golding.

★
EVERARDS TIGER

A mid-brown, well balanced best Bitter crafted for broad appeal, benefiting from a long, bitter-sweet finish.

ORIGINAL GRAVITY

1041

	19 litres	23 litres	25 litres
Pale Malt (grams)	2810	3400	3700
Crystal Malt (grams)	295	355	385
White Sugar (grams)	165	205	220
Torrefied Wheat (grams)	100	120	130
Black Malt (grams)	10	12	13
Start of Boil			
Challenger Hops (grams)	25	30	33
Last Ten Minutes of Boil			
Fuggle Hops (grams)	8	10	11
Irish Moss (grams)	3	3	3
Total liquor (litres)	26.6	32.2	35
Mash liquor (litres)	8	9.7	10.5

Mash schedule 66°C (151°F), 90 minutes

Boil time 90 minutes

Final gravity 1008

Alcohol content (ABV) 4.2%

Bitterness units (EBU) 26

Colour (EBC) 26

 Dry hop with a few cones of Golding.

EXE VALLEY AUTUMN GLORY

Nutty malt and peppery hop aromas. Full and rich dark malt in
the mouth, lingering finish with ripe malt and tangy bitter hops.
Well-rounded, good malt character, slightly burnt finish, ruby coloured.

ORIGINAL GRAVITY
1045

	19 litres	23 litres	25 litres
Pale Malt (grams)	3550	4300	4670
Crystal Malt (grams)	265	320	350
Start of Boil			
Fuggle Hops (grams)	29	35	38
Golding Hops (grams)	29	35	38
Last Ten Minutes of Boil			
Styrian Golding Hops (grams)	19	23	25
Irish Moss (grams)	3	3	3
Total liquor (litres)	27.1	32.9	35.7
Mash liquor (litres)	9.5	11.6	12.6

Mash schedule 66°C (151°F), 90 minutes

Boil time 90 minutes

Final gravity 1011

Alcohol content (ABV) 4.5%

Bitterness units (EBU) 42

Colour (EBC) 21

Malt extract version – Replace the pale malt with the appropriate quantity of pale-
coloured, premium-grade malt extract and brew using the malt extract brewing method.

	19 litres	23 litres	25 litres
Malt Extract Syrup (grams)	2660	3230	3500
or			
Dried Malt Extract (grams)	2290	2770	3010

★
EXE VALLEY DOB'S BEST BITTER

Light-brown Bitter. Malt and fruit predominate in the aroma and taste with a dry, bitter, fruity finish.

ORIGINAL GRAVITY
1040

	19 litres	23 litres	25 litres
Pale Malt (grams)	3220	3900	4230
Crystal Malt (grams)	165	205	220
Start of Boil			
Fuggle Hops (grams)	26	32	35
Golding Hops (grams)	26	32	35
Last Ten Minutes of Boil			
Golding Hops (grams)	18	21	23
Irish Moss (grams)	3	3	3
Total liquor (litres)	26.7	32.4	35.2
Mash liquor (litres)	8.5	10.3	11.1

Mash schedule 66°C (151°F), 90 minutes
Boil time 90 minutes
Final gravity 1010
Alcohol content (ABV) 4%
Bitterness units (EBU) 40
Colour (EBC) 15

Dry hop with a few cones of Golding.

. . . .

Malt extract version – Replace the pale malt with the appropriate quantity of pale-coloured, premium-grade malt extract and brew using the malt extract brewing method.

	19 litres	23 litres	25 litres
Malt Extract Syrup (grams)	2420	2930	3170
or			
Dried Malt Extract (grams)	2080	2520	2730

EXE VALLEY SPRING BEER

Pale gold beer with superb hop character; a seasonal brew
available between March and May. Massive resiny, floral and
citric hop aromas. Smooth malt and vanilla in the mouth;
finish becomes dry and bitter with tart citric notes.

ORIGINAL GRAVITY

1042

	19 litres	23 litres	25 litres
Pale Malt (grams)	3540	4280	4650
Start of Boil			
Target Hops (grams)	24	29	32
Last Ten Minutes of Boil			
Irish Moss (grams)	3	3	3
Post-boil Hops			
Styrian Golding Hops (grams)	5	6	6
Total liquor (litres)	26.9	32.6	35.4
Mash liquor (litres)	8.8	10.7	11.6

Mash schedule 66°C (151°F), 90 minutes
Boil time 90 minutes
Final gravity 1010
Alcohol content (ABV) 4.2%
Bitterness units (EBU) 38
Colour (EBC) 7

 Dry hop with a few cones of Golding.

Malt extract version – Replace the pale malt with the appropriate quantity of pale-
coloured, premium-grade malt extract and brew using the malt extract brewing method.

	19 litres	23 litres	25 litres
Malt Extract Syrup (grams)	2660	3210	3490
or			
Dried Malt Extract (grams)	2280	2760	3000

★
EXMOOR ALE

A pale to mid-brown, medium-bodied session Bitter.
A mixture of malt and hops in the aroma and taste lead
to a hoppy, bitter aftertaste.

ORIGINAL GRAVITY
1039

	19 litres	23 litres	25 litres
Pale Malt (grams)	3020	3660	3980
Crystal Malt (grams)	270	325	355
Chocolate Malt (grams)	23	28	31
Start of Boil			
Challenger Hops (grams)	37	45	49
Last Ten Minutes of Boil			
Irish Moss (grams)	3	3	3
Post-boil Hops			
Styrian Golding Hops (grams)	7	9	10
Total liquor (litres)	26.6	32.3	35.1
Mash liquor (litres)	8.2	10	10.8

Mash schedule 66°C (151°F), 90 minutes
Boil time 90 minutes
Final gravity 1010
Alcohol content (ABV) 3.8%
Bitterness units (EBU) 40
Colour (EBC) 30

• •

Malt extract version – Replace the pale malt with the appropriate quantity of pale-coloured, premium-grade malt extract and brew using the malt extract brewing method.

	19 litres	23 litres	25 litres
Malt Extract Syrup (grams)	2270	2750	2990
or			
Dried Malt Extract (grams)	1950	2360	2570

★
EXMOOR BEAST

A dark brown beer with a full palate. The maltiness on the
tongue is followed by a burst of hops with a lingering
bitter-sweet aftertaste.

ORIGINAL GRAVITY
1066

	19 litres	23 litres	25 litres
Pale Malt (grams)	4980	6020	6550
Crystal Malt (grams)	450	545	590
Chocolate Malt (grams)	205	250	270
Start of Boil			
Challenger Hops (grams)	47	57	62
Last Ten Minutes of Boil			
Brewers Gold Hops (grams)	16	19	21
Irish Moss (grams)	3	3	3
Total liquor (litres)	28.9	35.1	38.1
Mash liquor (litres)	14.1	17.1	18.5

Mash schedule 66°C (151°F), 90 minutes
Boil time 90 minutes
Final gravity 1017
Alcohol content (ABV) 6.5%
Bitterness units (EBU) 40
Colour (EBC) 119

Malt extract version – Replace the pale malt with the appropriate quantity of pale-
coloured, premium grade malt extract and brew using the malt extract brewing method.

	19 litres	23 litres	25 litres
Malt Extract Syrup (grams)	3735	4520	4910
or			
Dried Malt Extract (grams)	3210	3880	4230

EXMOOR GOLD

A yellow/golden best Bitter with a good balance of malt and
fruity hop on the nose and the palate. The sweetness
follows through an ultimately more bitter finish.

ORIGINAL GRAVITY
1045

	19 litres	23 litres	25 litres
Pale Malt (grams)	3790	4590	4980
Start of Boil			
Challenger Hops (grams)	39	47	51
Last Ten Minutes of Boil			
Golding Hops (grams)	13	16	17
Irish Moss (grams)	3	3	3
Post-boil Hops			
Styrian Golding Hops (grams)	8	9	10
Total liquor (litres)	27.1	32.9	35.7
Mash liquor (litres)	9.5	11.5	12.5

Mash schedule 66°C (151°F), 90 minutes
Boil time 90 minutes
Final gravity 1010
Alcohol content (ABV) 4.6%
Bitterness units (EBU) 40
Colour (EBC) 8

Malt extract version – Replace the pale malt with the appropriate quantity of pale-
coloured, premium grade malt extract and brew using the malt extract brewing method.

	19 litres	23 litres	25 litres
Malt Extract Syrup (grams)	2840	3440	3740
or			
Dried Malt Extract (grams)	2450	2960	3210

FELINFOEL BEST BITTER

A balanced beer with a low aroma. Bitter-sweet
initially with an increasing moderate bitterness.

ORIGINAL GRAVITY
1036

	19 litres	23 litres	25 litres
Pale Malt (grams)	2340	2830	3080
Torrefied Wheat (grams)	230	280	305
White Sugar (grams)	230	280	305
Crystal Malt (grams)	87	105	115
Black Malt (grams)	20	25	27
Start of Boil			
Challenger Hops (grams)	17	20	22
Bramling Cross Hops (grams)	6	7	8
Whitbread Golding Hops (grams)	6	7	8
Last Ten Minutes of Boil			
Whitbread Golding Hops (grams)	9	11	12
Irish Moss (grams)	3	3	3
Total liquor (litres)	26	31.5	34.2
Mash liquor (litres)	6.6	8.1	8.8

Mash schedule 66°C (151°F), 90 minutes

Boil time 90 minutes

Final gravity 1007

Alcohol content (ABV) 3.8%

Bitterness units (EBU) 28

Colour (EBC) 20

FELINFOEL DOUBLE DRAGON

This pale brown beer has a malty, fruity aroma.
The taste is also malt and fruit with a background hop
presence throughout. A malty and fruity finish.

ORIGINAL GRAVITY
1040

	19 litres	23 litres	25 litres
Pale Malt (grams)	2610	3160	3430
Torrefied Wheat (grams)	260	310	340
White Sugar (grams)	240	295	320
Crystal Malt (grams)	97	115	125
Black Malt (grams)	39	47	51

Start of Boil

Challenger Hops (grams)	18	22	24
Bramling Cross Hops (grams)	6	7	8
Whitbread Golding Hops (grams)	6	7	8

Last Ten Minutes of Boil

Whitbread Hops (grams)	10	12	13
Irish Moss (grams)	3	3	3

Total liquor (litres)	26.3	31.9	34.6
Mash liquor (litres)	7.5	9.1	9.8

Mash schedule 66°C (151°F), 90 minutes
Boil time 90 minutes
Final gravity 1008
Alcohol content (ABV) 4.2%
Bitterness units (EBU) 30
Colour (EBC) 31

FLOWERS IPA

Easy drinking session ale now brewed by Hall & Woodhouse. Light, spicy hop aroma. Malty bitterness with a long, citrus hop finish.

ORIGINAL GRAVITY
1035

	19 litres	23 litres	25 litres
Pale Malt (grams)	2370	2870	3120
White Sugar (grams)	225	270	295
Crystal Malt (grams)	210	255	275
Black Malt (grams)	17	21	22

Start of Boil

Target Hops (grams)	14	17	19

Last Ten Minutes of Boil

Styrian Golding Hops (grams)	5	6	6
Irish Moss (grams)	3	3	3

Total liquor (litres)	26	31.5	34.2
Mash liquor (litres)	6.5	7.9	8.5

Mash schedule 66°C (151°F), 90 minutes
Boil time 90 minutes
Final gravity 1007
Alcohol content (ABV) 3.7%
Bitterness units (EBU) 24
Colour (EBC) 24

Malt extract version – Replace the pale malt with the appropriate quantity of pale-coloured, premium grade malt extract and brew using the malt extract brewing method.

	19 litres	23 litres	25 litres
Malt Extract Syrup (grams)	1780	2150	2340
or			
Dried Malt Extract (grams)	1530	1850	2010

FLOWERS ORIGINAL

A strong, fruity Bitter with some acidity, now brewed by Hall & Wood-house under contract to InBev. Fat malt in the mouth with hop edge, dry finish with some hop character with raisin and sultana notes.

ORIGINAL GRAVITY
1040

	19 litres	23 litres	25 litres
Pale Malt (grams)	2710	3280	3560
White Sugar (grams)	255	310	340
Crystal Malt (grams)	240	290	315
Black Malt (grams)	19	23	26
Start of Boil			
Target Hops (grams)	17	20	22
Last Ten Minutes of Boil			
Styrian Golding Hops (grams)	6	7	7
Irish Moss (grams)	3	3	3
Total liquor (litres)	26.3	31.9	34.6
Mash liquor (litres)	7.4	9	9.7

Mash schedule 66°C (151°F), 90 minutes

Boil time 90 minutes

Final gravity 1007

Alcohol content (ABV) 4.4%

Bitterness units (EBU) 27

Colour (EBC) 28

 Dry hop with a few cones of Styrian Golding.

• •

Malt extract version Replace the pale malt with the appropriate quantity of pale-coloured, premium grade malt extract and brew using the malt extract brewing method.

	19 litres	23 litres	25 litres
Malt Extract Syrup (grams)	2030	2460	2670
or			
Dried Malt Extract (grams)	1750	2120	2300

★
FULLER'S DISCOVERY

This dark-gold beer has an aroma of citrus with slight perfume notes. The palate has the same fruit, complemented by malt and a dry finish.

ORIGINAL GRAVITY
1038

	19 litres	23 litres	25 litres
Pale Malt (grams)	2590	3130	3410
Wheat Malt (grams)	475	580	630
Crystal Malt (grams)	140	170	185
Start of Boil			
Liberty Hops (grams)	34	41	45
Last Ten Minutes of Boil			
Saaz Hops (grams)	11	14	15
Irish Moss (grams)	3	3	3
Post-boil Hops			
Saaz Hops (grams)	7	8	9
Total liquor (litres)	26.5	32.1	34.8
Mash liquor (litres)	7.7	9.4	10.2

Mash schedule 66°C (151°F), 90 minutes

Boil time 90 minutes

Final gravity 1009

Alcohol content (ABV) 3.7%

Bitterness units (EBU) 22

Colour (EBC) 13

 Dry hop with a few cones of Golding.

FULLER'S ESB

Inviting complex aroma. Flavours of fruity marmalade mixed with mixed with malt and hops, which remain in the dry finish with a hint of roast.

ORIGINAL GRAVITY
1054

	19 litres	23 litres	25 litres
Pale Malt (grams)	4180	5060	5500
Crystal Malt (grams)	410	500	540

Start of Boil

Target Hops (grams)	14	17	19
Challenger Hops (grams)	7	9	10
Northdown Hops (grams)	7	9	10

Last Ten Minutes of Boil

Golding Hops (grams)	10	12	13
Irish Moss (grams)	3	3	3

Total liquor (litres)	28	33.9	36.8
Mash liquor (litres)	11.4	13.9	15.1

Mash schedule 66°C (151°F), 90 minutes
Boil time 90 minutes
Final gravity 1013
Alcohol content (ABV) 5.4%
Bitterness units (EBU) 35
Colour (EBC) 30

 Dry hop with a few cones of Golding.

· ·

Malt extract version – Replace the pale malt with the appropriate quantity of pale-coloured, premium-grade malt extract and brew using the malt extract brewing method.

	19 litres	23 litres	25 litres
Malt Extract Syrup (grams)	3140	3800	4130
or			
Dried Malt Extract (grams)	2700	3260	3550

FULLER'S LONDON PRIDE

A fruity sweet malt nose with a hoppy edge that is also present on the palate and aftertaste; mellow peachy/orange notes give way to lingering dry, bitter aftertaste.

ORIGINAL GRAVITY

1040

	19 litres	23 litres	25 litres
Pale Malt (grams)	3100	3750	4080
Crystal Malt (grams)	305	370	400
Start of Boil			
Target Hops (grams)	11	13	14
Challenger Hops (grams)	6	7	8
Northdown Hops (grams)	6	7	8
Last Ten Minutes of Boil			
Golding Hops (grams)	7	9	10
Irish Moss (grams)	3	3	3
Total liquor (litres)	26.7	32.4	35.2
Mash liquor (litres)	8.5	10.3	11.1

Mash schedule 66°C (151°F), 90 minutes

Boil time 90 minutes

Final gravity 1010

Alcohol content (ABV) 4%

Bitterness units (EBU) 30

Colour (EBC) 22

 Dry hop with a few cones of Golding.

Malt extract version – Replace the pale malt with the appropriate quantity of pale-coloured, premium-grade malt extract and brew using the malt extract brewing method.

	19 litres	23 litres	25 litres
Malt Extract Syrup (grams)	2330	2810	3060
or			
Dried Malt Extract (grams)	2000	2420	2630

★
GALE'S BUTSER BITTER

A red-chestnut coloured beer from Gale's Horndean brewery.
Delicate aroma of hops and hints of fruit. Full malt
flavour balanced by fruit and a lingering hop finish.

ORIGINAL GRAVITY
1034

	19 litres	23 litres	25 litres
Pale Malt (grams)	2360	2860	3110
Torrefied Wheat (grams)	195	235	255
White Sugar (grams	140	170	180
Crystal Malt (grams)	70	85	92
Black Malt (grams)	34	41	44
Start of Boil			
Challenger Hops (grams)	13	16	17
Fuggle Hops (grams)	9	11	12
Last Ten Minutes of Boil			
Golding Hops (grams)	7	9	10
Irish Moss (grams)	3	3	3
Total liquor (litres)	26	31.5	34.2
Mash liquor (litres)	6.6	8.1	8.8

Mash schedule 66°C (151°F), 90 minutes

Boil time 90 minutes

Final gravity 1007

Alcohol content (ABV) 3.6%

Bitterness units (EBU) 21

Colour (EBC) 26

GALE'S HSB

A complex, slightly sour strong ale from the Gale's Horndean brewery, near Portsmouth. Full malt with hop edge in the mouth, intense finish with citric and faint chocolate notes.

ORIGINAL GRAVITY

1050

	19 litres	23 litres	25 litres
Pale Malt (grams)	3490	4230	4600
Torrified Wheat (grams)	245	295	325
White Sugar (grams)	205	245	270
Crystal Malt (grams)	120	150	160
Black Malt (grams)	45	55	60

Start of Boil

	19 litres	23 litres	25 litres
Challenger Hops (grams)	18	22	24
Fuggle Hops (grams)	12	15	16

Last Ten Minutes of Boil

	19 litres	23 litres	25 litres
Golding Hops (grams)	10	12	13
Irish Moss (grams)	3	3	3

	19 litres	23 litres	25 litres
Total liquor (litres)	27.2	33	35.8
Mash liquor (litres)	9.7	11.8	12.8

Mash schedule 66°C (151°F), 90 minutes

Boil time 90 minutes

Final gravity 1010

Alcohol content (ABV) 5.3%

Bitterness units (EBU) 26

Colour (EBC) 37

★
HARVIESTOUN PTARMIGAN

A well-balanced bitter-sweet beer in which malt and
hops dominate. The blend of malt, hops and fruit
produces a clean, hoppy aftertaste.

ORIGINAL GRAVITY
1045

	19 litres	23 litres	25 litres
Pale Malt (grams)	3340	4050	4400
Wheat Malt (grams)	145	180	195
Crystal Malt (grams)	110	135	145
White Sugar (grams)	110	135	145
Black Malt (grams)	11	14	15
Start of Boil			
Challenger Hops (grams)	33	40	44
Last Ten Minutes of Boil			
Saaz Hops (grams)	11	13	14
Irish Moss (grams)	3	3	3
Total liquor (litres)	27	32.7	35.5
Mash liquor (litres)	9	10.9	11.8

Mash schedule 66°C (151°F), 90 minutes

Boil time 90 minutes

Final gravity 1010

Alcohol content (ABV) 4.6%

Bitterness units (EBU) 34

Colour (EBC) 18

HOOK NORTON HOOKY BITTER

A classic golden session Bitter. Hoppy and fruity aroma
followed by a malt and hops taste and a continuing hoppy finish.

ORIGINAL GRAVITY
1035

	19 litres	23 litres	25 litres
Pale Malt (grams)	2110	2550	2770
Flaked Maize (grams)	280	340	370
White Sugar (grams)	225	270	295
Crystal Malt (grams)	165	200	220
Black Malt (grams)	28	34	37

Start of Boil

Challenger Hops (grams)	20	24	26

Last Ten Minutes of Boil

Fuggle Hops (grams)	7	8	9
Irish Moss (grams)	3	3	3

Total liquor (litres)	25.9	31.4	34.1
Mash liquor (litres)	6.4	7.8	8.4

Mash schedule 66°C (151°F), 90 minutes
Boil time 90 minutes
Final gravity 1007
Alcohol content (ABV) 3.7%
Bitterness units (EBU) 22
Colour (EBC) 27

 Dry hop with a few cones of Golding.

HOOK NORTON OLD HOOKY

A strong Bitter, tawny in colour. A well-rounded fruity taste with a balanced bitter finish.

ORIGINAL GRAVITY
1042

	19 litres	23 litres	25 litres
Pale Malt (grams)	2530	3060	3330
Flaked Maize (grams)	335	405	440
White Sugar (grams)	270	325	355
Crystal Malt (grams)	200	245	265
Black Malt (grams)	34	41	44
Start of Boil			
Challenger Hops (grams)	29	35	38
Last Ten Minutes of Boil			
Fuggle Hops (grams)	10	12	13
Irish Moss (grams)	3	3	3
Total liquor (litres)	26.5	32.1	34.8
Mash liquor (litres)	7.7	9.4	10.2

Mash schedule 66°C (151°F), 90 minutes

Boil time 90 minutes

Final gravity 1008

Alcohol content (ABV) 4.5%

Bitterness units (EBU) 30

Colour (EBC) 33

 Dry hop with a few cones of Golding.

PALE ALE & BITTER RECIPES

HOP BACK SUMMER LIGHTNING

A pleasurable pale Bitter with a good, fresh, hoppy aroma and a malty, hoppy flavour. Finely balanced, it has an intense bitterness, leading to a long, dry finish.

ORIGINAL GRAVITY
1049

	19 litres	23 litres	25 litres
Pale Malt (grams)	4120	4990	5430

Start of Boil

	19 litres	23 litres	25 litres
Challenger Hops (grams)	38	46	50

Last Ten Minutes of Boil

	19 litres	23 litres	25 litres
Golding Hops (grams)	13	15	17
Irish Moss (grams)	3	3	3

Post-boil Hops

	19 litres	23 litres	25 litres
Golding Hops (grams)	8	9	10

	19 litres	23 litres	25 litres
Total liquor (litres)	27.5	33.3	36.1
Mash liquor (litres)	10.3	12.5	13.5

Mash schedule 66°C (151°F), 90 minutes
Boil time 90 minutes
Final gravity 1011
Alcohol content (ABV) 5%
Bitterness units (EBU) 38
Colour (EBC) 8

Malt extract version – Replace the pale malt with the appropriate quantity of pale-coloured, premium-grade malt extract and brew using the malt extract brewing method.

	19 litres	23 litres	25 litres
Malt Extract Syrup (grams)	3090	3740	4070
or			
Dried Malt Extract (grams)	2660	3220	3500

★
HYDES ORIGINAL BITTER

Pale brown beer with a malty nose, malt and an earthy
hoppiness in the taste, and a good bitterness through to the finish.

ORIGINAL GRAVITY
1035

	19 litres	23 litres	25 litres
Pale Malt (grams)	2820	3410	3710
Crystal Malt (grams)	115	140	155
Black Malt (grams)	24	29	31
Start of Boil			
Challenger Hops (grams)	26	31	34
Last Ten Minutes of Boil			
Fuggle Hops (grams)	9	10	11
Irish Moss (grams)	3	3	3
Total liquor (litres)	26.3	31.9	34.6
Mash liquor (litres)	7.4	9	9.7

Mash schedule 66°C (151°F), 90 minutes
Boil time 90 minutes
Final gravity 1009
Alcohol content (ABV) 3.4%
Bitterness units (EBU) 28
Colour (EBC) 24

Dry hop with a few cones of Fuggles.

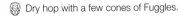

Malt extract version – Replace the pale malt with the appropriate quantity of pale-
coloured, premium-grade malt extract and brew using the malt extract brewing method.

	19 litres	23 litres	25 litres
Malt Extract Syrup (grams)	2120	2560	2780
or			
Dried Malt Extract (grams)	1820	2120	2390

J.W. LEES BITTER

Pale brown beer with a malty, hoppy aroma.
Distinctive malty, dry flavour and aftertaste.

ORIGINAL GRAVITY
1037

	19 litres	23 litres	25 litres
Pale Malt (grams)	3090	3740	4070
Chocolate Malt (grams)	28	34	37

Start of Boil

Golding Hops (grams)	34	41	45

Last Ten Minutes of Boil

Golding Hops (grams)	11	14	15
Irish Moss (grams)	3	3	3

Total liquor (litres)	26.5	32.1	34.8
Mash liquor (litres)	7.7	9.4	10.2

Mash schedule 66°C (151°F), 90 minutes
Boil time 90 minutes
Final gravity 1009
Alcohol content (ABV) 3.7%
Bitterness units (EBU) 28
Colour (EBC) 18

 Dry hop with a few cones of Golding.

Malt extract version – Replace the pale malt with the appropriate quantity of pale-coloured, premium-grade malt extract and brew using the malt extract brewing method.

	19 litres	23 litres	25 litres
Malt Extract Syrup (grams)	2320	2810	3050
or			
Dried Malt Extract (grams)	1990	2410	2630

★
J.W. LEES MOONRAKER

A reddish-brown beer with a strong, malty, fruity aroma. The flavour is rich and sweet, with roast malt, and the finish is fruity yet dry.

ORIGINAL GRAVITY
1073

	19 litres	23 litres	25 litres
Pale Malt (grams)	6000	7260	7890
Chocolate Malt (grams)	165	200	215
Start of Boil			
Golding Hops (grams)	50	61	66
Last Ten Minutes of Boil			
Golding Hops (grams)	17	20	22
Irish Moss (grams)	3	3	3
Total liquor (litres)	29.5	35.8	38.9
Mash liquor (litres)	15.4	18.7	20.3

Mash schedule 66°C (151°F), 90 minutes
Boil time 90 minutes
Final gravity 1018
Alcohol content (ABV) 7.3%
Bitterness units (EBU) 30
Colour (EBC) 80

Malt extract version – Replace the pale malt with the appropriate quantity of pale-coloured, premium-grade malt extract and brew using the malt extract brewing method.

	19 litres	23 litres	25 litres
Malt Extract Syrup (grams)	4500	5450	5920
or			
Dried Malt Extract (grams)	3870	4680	5090

JENNINGS COCKER HOOP

A rich, creamy, gold-coloured Bitter with good hop appeal. Good hop aroma with fruit notes. Initial complex taste of hop, fruit and malt followed by a refreshing hoppy and bitter finish.

ORIGINAL GRAVITY
1046

	19 litres	23 litres	25 litres
Pale Malt (grams)	3500	4230	4600
Torrefied Wheat (grams)	390	470	515
Black Malt (grams)	24	28	31
Start of Boil			
Challenger Hops (grams)	35	42	46
Last Ten Minutes of Boil			
Styrian Golding Hops (grams)	12	14	15
Irish Moss (grams)	3	3	3
Post-boil Hops			
Styrian Golding Hops (grams)	7	8	9
Total liquor (litres)	27.2	33	35.8
Mash liquor (litres)	9.7	11.8	12.8

Mash schedule 66°C (151°F), 90 minutes
Boil time 90 minutes
Final gravity 1011
Alcohol content (ABV) 4.6%
Bitterness units (EBU) 35
Colour (EBC) 20

JENNINGS CUMBERLAND ALE

A light, creamy, hoppy beer with a dry aftertaste.

ORIGINAL GRAVITY
1038

	19 litres	23 litres	25 litres
Pale Malt (grams)	2440	2950	3210
Torrefied Wheat (grams)	305	365	400
White Sugar (grams)	270	330	360
Black Malt (grams)	31	37	40
Start of Boil			
Challenger Hops (grams)	27	33	36
Last Ten Minutes of Boil			
Golding Hops (grams)	9	11	12
Irish Moss (grams)	3	3	3
Total liquor (litres)	26.1	31.7	34.4
Mash liquor (litres)	6.9	8.4	9.1

Mash schedule 66°C (151°F), 90 minutes

Boil time 90 minutes

Final gravity 1007

Alcohol content (ABV) 4.1%

Bitterness units (EBU) 30

Colour (EBC) 21

PALE ALE & BITTER RECIPES

MARSTONS BURTON BITTER

Overwhelming sulphurous aroma supports a scattering of hops and fruit with an easy-drinking sweetness. Suddenly the taste develops from a sweet middle to a satisfyingly hoppy finish.

ORIGINAL GRAVITY
1036

	19 litres	23 litres	25 litres
Pale Malt (grams)	2700	3270	3550
White Sugar (grams)	175	210	230
Black Malt (grams)	44	53	58
Start of Boil			
Whitbread Golding Hops (grams)	22	26	28
Fuggle Hops (grams)	14	17	19
Last Ten Minutes of Boil			
Golding Hops (grams)	12	14	15
Irish Moss (grams)	3	3	3
Total liquor (litres)	26.1	31.6	34.3
Mash liquor (litres)	6.8	8.3	9

Mash schedule 66°C (151°F), 90 minutes

Boil time 90 minutes

Final gravity 1007

Alcohol content (ABV) 3.8%

Bitterness units (EBU) 30

Colour (EBC) 28

 Dry hop with a few cones of Golding.

• •

Malt extract version – Replace the pale malt with the appropriate quantity of pale-coloured, premium-grade malt extract and brew using the malt extract brewing method.

	19 litres	23 litres	25 litres
Malt Extract Syrup (grams)	2030	2450	2660
or			
Dried Malt Extract (grams)	1740	2110	2290

MARSTONS PEDIGREE

Sweet beer with a slight sulphur aroma. Has the hoppy but sweet sensation of a short session beer.

ORIGINAL GRAVITY
1043

	19 litres	23 litres	25 litres
Pale Malt (grams)	2910	3520	3830
White Sugar (grams)	400	485	530
Black Malt (grams)	47	57	62
Start of Boil			
Whitbread Golding Hops (grams)	26	32	35
Fuggle Hops (grams)	17	21	23
Last Ten Minutes of Boil			
Whitbread Golding Hops (grams)	15	18	19
Irish Moss (grams)	3	3	3
Total liquor (litres)	26.3	31.9	34.6
Mash liquor (litres)	7.3	8.9	9.6

Mash schedule 66°C (151°F), 90 minutes
Boil time 90 minutes
Final gravity 1007
Alcohol content (ABV) 4.8%
Bitterness units (EBU) 35
Colour (EBC) 30

 Dry hop with a few cones of Golding.

Malt extract version – Replace the pale malt with the appropriate quantity of pale-coloured, premium-grade malt extract and brew using the malt extract brewing method.

	19 litres	23 litres	25 litres
Malt Extract Syrup (grams)	2180	2640	2870
or			
Dried Malt Extract (grams)	1880	2270	2470

MCMULLEN COUNTRY BEST BITTER

A full-bodied beer with a well-balanced mix of malt,
hops and fruit throughout.

ORIGINAL GRAVITY
1040

	19 litres	23 litres	25 litres
Pale Malt (grams)	2990	3620	3940
White Sugar (grams)	160	195	215
Crystal Malt (grams)	98	115	125
Black Malt (grams)	16	20	22

Start of Boil

	19 litres	23 litres	25 litres
Bramling Cross Hops (grams)	17	21	22
Progress Hops (grams)	17	20	22

Last Ten Minutes of Boil

	19 litres	23 litres	25 litres
Fuggle Hops (grams)	11	14	15
Irish Moss (grams)	3	3	3
Total liquor (litres)	26.5	32.1	34.8
Mash liquor (litres)	7.7	9.4	10.2

Mash schedule 66°C (151°F), 90 minutes
Boil time 90 minutes
Final gravity 1008
Alcohol content (ABV) 4.2%
Bitterness units (EBU) 30
Colour (EBC) 19

Malt extract version – Replace the pale malt with the appropriate quantity of pale-coloured, premium-grade malt extract and brew using the malt extract brewing method.

	19 litres	23 litres	25 litres
Malt Extract Syrup (grams)	2240	2720	2960
or			
Dried Malt Extract (grams)	1930	2340	2540

MOORHOUSES PENDLE WITCHES BREW

A deceptively pale strong Bitter, dangerously potable.
Sweet grain in the mouth, deep, dry finish with
good hop character and vanilla notes.

ORIGINAL GRAVITY
1048

	19 litres	23 litres	25 litres
Pale Malt (grams)	3130	3790	4120
Crystal Malt (grams)	310	375	410
White Sugar (grams)	270	330	360
Torrefied Wheat (grams)	195	235	255
Start of Boil			
Fuggle Hops (grams)	46	56	61
Last Ten Minutes of Boil			
Irish Moss (grams)	3	3	3
Post-boil Hops			
Fuggle Hops (grams)	9	11	12
Total liquor (litres)	27	32.7	35.5
Mash liquor (litres)	9	11	11.9

Mash schedule 66°C (151°F), 90 minutes

Boil time 90 minutes

Final gravity 1009

Alcohol content (ABV) 5.2%

Bitterness units (EBU) 30

Colour (EBC) 23

★
MORLAND OLD SPECKLED HEN

Richly coloured and fruit flavoured strong ale with generous hop support. Superb floral Goldings hop aroma. Full malt and hops in the mouth; long dry finish with hops and delicate fruit notes.

ORIGINAL GRAVITY
1050

	19 litres	23 litres	25 litres
Pale Malt (grams)	3130	3780	4110
White Sugar (grams)	470	570	620
Crystal Malt (grams)	315	380	410
Black Malt (grams)	24	29	31

Start of Boil

	19 litres	23 litres	25 litres
Challenger Hops (grams)	32	39	42

Last Ten Minutes of Boil

	19 litres	23 litres	25 litres
Golding Hops (grams)	11	13	14
Irish Moss (grams)	3	3	3

	19 litres	23 litres	25 litres
Total liquor (litres)	26.8	32.5	35.3
Mash liquor (litres)	8.6	10.5	11.4

Mash schedule 66°C (151°F), 90 minutes
Boil time 90 minutes
Final gravity 1008
Alcohol content (ABV) 5.6%
Bitterness units (EBU) 32
Colour (EBC) 35

Malt extract version – Replace the pale malt with the appropriate quantity of pale-coloured, premium-grade malt extract and brew using the malt extract brewing method.

	19 litres	23 litres	25 litres
Malt Extract Syrup (grams)	2350	2840	3080
or			
Dried Malt Extract (grams)	2020	2440	2650

RINGWOOD BEST BITTER

Easy-drinking, slightly tart pale Bitter. Tempting hop aroma with light fruit notes. Strong malt and hop flavours with dry, tangy, fruit finish.

ORIGINAL GRAVITY
1038

	19 litres	23 litres	25 litres
Pale Malt (grams)	2910	3530	3830
Crystal Malt (grams)	160	195	210
Torrefied Wheat (grams)	125	155	170
Chocolate Malt (grams)	29	35	38
Start of Boil			
Challenger Hops (grams)	22	27	29
Last Ten Minutes of Boil			
Golding Hops (grams)	7	9	10
Irish Moss (grams)	3	3	3
Total liquor (litres)	26.6	32.2	35
Mash liquor (litres)	8	9.8	10.6

Mash schedule 66°C (151°F), 90 minutes

Boil time 90 minutes

Final gravity 1009

Alcohol content (ABV) 3.8%

Bitterness units (EBU) 24

Colour (EBC) 26

RINGWOOD FORTYNINER

A mid-brown beer. A fruity aroma with some malt leads to a sweet but well-balanced taste with malt, fruit and citrus hop flavours all present. The finish is bitter-sweet with some fruit.

ORIGINAL GRAVITY
1049

	19 litres	23 litres	25 litres
Pale Malt (grams)	3890	4710	5120
Crystal Malt (grams)	165	200	215
Torrefied Wheat (grams)	83	100	105
Chocolate Malt (grams)	13	15	16
Start of Boil			
Challenger Hops (grams)	24	29	32
Last Ten Minutes of Boil			
Golding Hops (grams)	8	10	10
Irish Moss (grams)	3	3	3
Post-boil Hops			
Golding Hops (grams)	5	6	6
Total liquor (litres)	27.5	33.3	36.1
Mash liquor (litres)	10.4	12.6	13.6

Mash schedule 66°C (151°F), 90 minutes
Boil time 90 minutes
Final gravity 1012
Alcohol content (ABV) 4.9%
Bitterness units (EBU) 28
Colour (EBC) 22

RINGWOOD OLD THUMPER

A warm, rounded, yet surprisingly delicate, pale strong beer from Ringwood brewery in Hampshire. Voted Champion Beer of Britain in 1988. Luscious balance of grain and hop in the mouth. Bitter-sweet finish with pronounced hop aftertaste.

ORIGINAL GRAVITY
1056

	19 litres	23 litres	25 litres
Pale Malt (grams)	4260	5160	5610
Torrefied Wheat (grams)	285	345	375
Crystal Malt (grams)	190	230	250
Chocolate Malt (grams)	29	35	38
Start of Boil			
Challenger Hops (grams)	34	41	45
Last Ten Minutes of Boil			
Golding Hops (grams)	11	14	15
Irish Moss (grams)	3	3	3
Post-boil Hops			
Golding Hops (grams)	7	8	9
Total liquor (litres)	28.1	34.1	37
Mash liquor (litres)	11.8	14.4	15.6

Mash schedule 66°C (151°F), 90 minutes
Boil time 90 minutes
Final gravity 1013
Alcohol content (ABV) 5.7%
Bitterness units (EBU) 32
Colour (EBC) 31

★
ROBINSONS OLD STOCKPORT

A beer with a refreshing taste of malt, hops and citrus fruit;
a fruity aroma and a short, dry finish. Not much 'old' about
it at 1035 though; I doubt if it gets to see a Sunday.

ORIGINAL GRAVITY
1035

	19 litres	23 litres	25 litres
Pale Malt (grams)	2590	3140	3410
Crystal Malt (grams)	205	250	270
Wheat Malt (grams)	145	180	195
Black Malt (grams)	21	25	27
Start of Boil			
Northdown Hops (grams)	25	30	33
Last Ten Minutes of Boil			
Golding Hops (grams)	8	10	11
Irish Moss (grams)	3	3	3
Total liquor (litres)	26.3	31.9	34.6
Mash liquor (litres)	7.4	9	9.7

Mash schedule 66°C (151°F), 90 minutes

Boil time 90 minutes

Final gravity 1009

Alcohol content (ABV) 3.4%

Bitterness units (EBU) 30

Colour (EBC) 27

★
ROBINSONS OLD TOM

A full-bodied dark beer with malt, fruit and chocolate in the aroma.
A delightfully complex range of flavours includes dark chocolate. Full
maltiness, port and fruit tastes lead to a long, bitter-sweet aftertaste.

ORIGINAL GRAVITY
1080

	19 litres	23 litres	25 litres
Pale Malt (grams)	5440	6580	7160
Crystal Malt (grams)	455	550	595
White Sugar (grams)	455	550	595
Chocolate Malt (grams)	155	185	205

Start of Boil

Whitbread Golding Hops (grams)	36	43	47
Golding Hops (grams)	23	28	30

Last Ten Minutes of Boil

Golding Hops (grams)	19	23	26
Irish Moss (grams)	3	3	3

Total liquor (litres)	24.9	35.6	38.6
Mash liquor (litres)	15.1	18.3	19.8

Mash schedule 66°C (151°F), 90 minutes
Boil time 90 minutes
Final gravity 1016
Alcohol content (ABV) 8.5%
Bitterness units (EBU) 35
Colour (EBC) 99

N.B. *Beware, the grist will be a tight fit in the average mash tun.*

• •

Malt extract version – Replace the pale malt with the appropriate quantity of pale-
coloured, premium-grade malt extract and brew using the malt extract brewing method.

	19 litres	23 litres	25 litres
Malt Extract Syrup (grams)	4160	4940	5370
or			
Dried Malt Extract (grams)	3570	4240	4618

RUDDLES BEST

An amber/brown beer, strong on bitterness but with some initial sweetness, fruit and subtle hop. Dryness lingers in the aftertaste.

ORIGINAL GRAVITY
1037

	19 litres	23 litres	25 litres
Pale Malt (grams)	2670	3240	3520
White Sugar (grams)	225	275	300
Black Malt (grams)	39	47	51
Crystal Malt (grams)	30	36	39

Start of Boil

	19 litres	23 litres	25 litres
Northdown Hops (grams)	20	24	26
Bramling Cross Hops (grams)	7	8	9
Fuggle Hops (grams)	7	8	9

Last Ten Minutes of Boil

	19 litres	23 litres	25 litres
Golding Hops (grams)	11	13	14
Irish Moss (grams)	3	3	3

Post-boil Hops

	19 litres	23 litres	25 litres
Golding Hops (grams)	7	8	9
Total liquor (litres)	26.1	31.6	34.3
Mash liquor (litres)	6.8	8.3	9

Mash schedule 66°C (151°F), 90 minutes
Boil time 90 minutes
Final gravity 1007
Alcohol content (ABV) 4%
Bitterness units (EBU) 35
Colour (EBC) 27

· ·

Malt extract version – Replace the pale malt with the appropriate quantity of pale-coloured, premium-grade malt extract and brew using the malt extract brewing method.

	19 litres	23 litres	25 litres
Malt Extract Syrup (grams)	2000	2430	2640
or			
Dried Malt Extract (grams)	1720	2090	2270

THEAKSTON BEST BITTER

Pale Bitter with distinctive hop flower character; quenching
and lightly fruity. Delicate bitter-sweet balance in the
mouth. Light dry finish with good hop character.

ORIGINAL GRAVITY
1038

	19 litres	23 litres	25 litres
Pale Malt (grams)	3040	3680	4000
Crystal Malt (grams)	175	210	230
Start of Boil			
Challenger Hops (grams)	17	20	22
Fuggle Hops	8	10	11
Last Ten Minutes of Boil			
Fuggle Hops (grams)	8	10	11
Irish Moss (grams)	3	3	3
Total liquor (litres)	26.6	32.2	35
Mash liquor (litres)	8	9.7	10.5

Mash schedule 66°C (151°F), 90 minutes

Boil time 90 minutes

Final gravity 1009

Alcohol content (ABV) 3.8 %

Bitterness units (EBU) 24

Colour (EBC) 15

 Dry hop with a few cones of Styrian Golding.

· ·

Malt extract version – Replace the pale malt with the appropriate quantity of pale-coloured, premium-grade malt extract and brew using the malt extract brewing method.

	19 litres	23 litres	25 litres
Malt Extract Syrup (grams)	2280	2760	3000
or			
Dried Malt Extract (grams)	1960	2370	2580

★
THEAKSTON OLD PECULIER

Dark and vinous old ale, bursting with complex fruit flavours. Massive winey bouquet of rich fruit with peppery hop notes. Toffee and roast malt in the mouth, deep bitter-sweet finish with delicate hops.

ORIGINAL GRAVITY
1058

	19 litres	23 litres	25 litres
Pale Malt (grams)	4510	5460	5930
Crystal Malt (grams)	245	295	325
Chocolate Malt (grams)	175	215	230

Start of Boil

	19 litres	23 litres	25 litres
Challenger Hops (grams)	24	29	32
Fuggle Hops (grams)	12	14	15

Last Ten Minutes of Boil

	19 litres	23 litres	25 litres
Golding Hops (grams)	12	14	15
Irish Moss (grams)	3	3	3

	19 litres	23 litres	25 litres
Total liquor (litres)	28.3	34.3	37.2
Mash liquor (litres)	12.3	14.9	16.1

Mash schedule 66°C (151°F), 90 minutes
Boil time 90 minutes
Final gravity 1015
Alcohol content (ABV) 5.7%
Bitterness units (EBU) 29
Colour (EBC) 95

 Dry hop with a few cones of Styrian Golding.

•••

Malt extract version – Replace the pale malt with the appropriate quantity of pale-coloured, premium grade malt extract and brew using the malt extract brewing method.

	19 litres	23 litres	25 litres
Malt Extract Syrup (grams)	3380	4100	4450
or			
Dried Malt Extract (grams)	2910	3520	3830

TIMOTHY TAYLOR BEST BITTER

A golden Bitter of exceptional quality and drinkability.
Full and complex grain and fruit with deep,
dry nutty finish.

ORIGINAL GRAVITY
1038

	19 litres	23 litres	25 litres
Pale Malt (grams)	3030	3670	3990
Crystal Malt (grams)	160	195	210
Black Malt (grams)	26	31	34
Start of Boil			
Golding Hops (grams)	35	42	46
Last Ten Minutes of Boil			
Golding Hops (grams)	12	14	15
Irish Moss (grams)	3	3	3
Total liquor (litres)	26.6	32.2	35
Mash liquor (litres)	8	9.8	10.6

Mash schedule 66°C (151°F), 90 minutes
Boil time 90 minutes
Final gravity 1009
Alcohol content (ABV) 3.8%
Bitterness units (EBU) 28
Colour (EBC) 27

Malt extract version – Replace the pale malt with the appropriate quantity of pale-
coloured, premium grade malt extract and brew using the malt extract brewing method.

	19 litres	23 litres	25 litres
Malt Extract Syrup (grams)	2270	2750	2990
or			
Dried Malt Extract (grams)	1950	2370	2570

TIMOTHY TAYLOR LANDLORD

A superb beer of enormous character and complexity, from the Knowl Spring brewery in Keighley. Stunning, mouth-filling, multi-layered interweaving of malt and hop with intense hop and fruit finish.

ORIGINAL GRAVITY
1042

	19 litres	23 litres	25 litres
Pale Malt (grams)	3510	4250	4620
Black Malt (grams)	25	30	33

Start of Boil

	19 litres	23 litres	25 litres
Golding Hops (grams)	25	30	33
Styrian Golding Hops (grams)	25	30	33

Last Ten Minutes of Boil

	19 litres	23 litres	25 litres
Styrian Golding Hops (grams)	16	20	22
Irish Moss (grams)	3	3	3

	19 litres	23 litres	25 litres
Total liquor (litres)	26.9	32.6	35.4
Mash liquor (litres)	8.8	10.7	11.6

Mash schedule 66°C (151°F), 90 minutes
Boil time 90 minutes
Final gravity 1010
Alcohol content (ABV) 4.2%
Bitterness units (EBU) 35
Colour (EBC) 20

Malt extract version – Replace the pale malt with the appropriate quantity of pale-coloured, premium grade malt extract and brew using the malt extract brewing method.

	19 litres	23 litres	25 litres
Malt Extract Syrup (grams)	2630	3120	3740
or			
Dried Malt Extract (grams)	2260	2740	2980

WADWORTH 6X

Copper-coloured ale with a malty and fruity nose, and some balancing hop character. The flavour is similar, with some bitterness and a lingering malty, but bitter finish. Full-bodied and distinctive.

ORIGINAL GRAVITY
1042

	19 litres	23 litres	25 litres
Pale Malt (grams)	3210	3890	4230
Crystal Malt (grams)	135	165	180
White Sugar (grams)	105	125	135
Black Malt (grams)	28	34	37

Start of Boil

Fuggle Hops (grams)	34	41	45

Last Ten Minutes of Boil

Irish Moss (grams)	3	3	3

Post-boil Hops

Golding Hops (grams)	7	8	9
Total liquor (litres)	26.7	32.4	35.2
Mash liquor (litres)	8.4	10.2	11

Mash schedule 66°C (151°F), 90 minutes
Boil time 90 minutes
Final gravity 1009
Alcohol content (ABV) 4.4%
Bitterness units (EBU) 23
Colour (EBC) 28

Malt extract version – Replace the pale malt with the appropriate quantity of pale-coloured, premium grade malt extract and brew using the malt extract brewing method.

	19 litres	23 litres	25 litres
Malt Extract Syrup (grams)	2410	2920	3170
or			
Dried Malt Extract (grams)	2070	2510	2730

WADWORTH JCB

A deep amber, robust but perfectly balanced traditional English ale with a rich, malty body, complex hop character and a hint of tropical fruit in the aroma and taste. A gentle barley-sugar sweetness blends wonderfully with smooth, nutty malt and rounded hop bitterness before a dry, biscuity, bitter finish.

ORIGINAL GRAVITY
1048

	19 litres	23 litres	25 litres
Pale Malt (grams)	3670	4440	4820
Crystal Malt (grams)	405	495	535
Black Malt (grams)	16	20	22
Start of Boil			
Fuggle Hops (grams)	25	30	33
Golding Hops (grams)	25	30	33
Last Ten Minutes of Boil			
Fuggle Hops (grams)	8	10	11
Golding Hops (grams)	8	10	11
Irish Moss (grams)	3	3	3
Total liquor (litres)	27.5	33.3	36.1
Mash liquor (litres)	10.2	12.4	13.4

Bring approximately 1 litre of water to the boil and turn off the heat. Infuse about 10 grams of hops in this hot water and leave to stand for an hour or so, while the main boil is taking place. Add this infusion, water and all, to the copper just before emptying.

Mash schedule 66°C (151°F), 90 minutes

Boil time 90 minutes

Final gravity 1012

Alcohol content (ABV) 4.8%

Bitterness units (EBU) 35

Colour (EBC) 37

Malt extract version – Replace the pale malt with the appropriate quantity of pale-coloured, premium grade malt extract and brew using the malt extract brewing method.

	19 litres	23 litres	25 litres
Malt Extract Syrup (grams)	2750	3330	3620
or			
Dried Malt Extract (grams)	2370	2860	3110

★
WADWORTH OLD FATHER TIMER

Aromatic winter beer. Ripe fruit and hop aromas. Full malt in the mouth, long finish full of hop bitterness with banana and sultana tones.

ORIGINAL GRAVITY
1056

	19 litres	23 litres	25 litres
Pale Malt (grams)	4280	5180	5630
Crystal Malt (grams)	185	225	245
White Sugar (grams)	140	165	180
Black Malt (grams)	42	51	55
Start of Boil			
Fuggle Hops (grams)	36	44	48
Last Ten Minutes of Boil			
Golding Hops (grams)	12	15	16
Irish Moss (grams)	3	3	3
Post-boil Hops			
Golding Hops (grams)	7	9	10
Total liquor (litres)	27.9	33.8	36.7
Mash liquor (litres)	11.3	13.7	14.8

Mash schedule 66°C (151°F), 90 minutes
Boil time 90 minutes
Final gravity 1012
Alcohol content (ABV) 5.8%
Bitterness units (EBU) 22
Colour (EBC) 40

Malt extract version – Replace the pale malt with the appropriate quantity of pale-coloured, premium grade malt extract and brew using the malt extract brewing method.

	19 litres	23 litres	25 litres
Malt Extract Syrup (grams)	3210	3890	4220
or			
Dried Malt Extract (grams)	2760	3340	3630

WORTHINGTON WHITE SHIELD

The classic India pale ale. A superb drink on its own or with meat,
fish and cheese dishes. Malt and spice in the mouth, deep nutty
finish with strong hop character and light apple fruit notes.

ORIGINAL GRAVITY
1050

	19 litres	23 litres	25 litres
Pale Malt (grams)	3300	4000	4350
White Sugar (grams)	395	480	520
Crystal Malt (grams)	275	335	365
Start of Boil			
Challenger Hops (grams)	23	28	30
Northdown Hops (grams)	16	19	21
Last Ten Minutes of Boil			
Northdown Hops (grams)	13	16	17
Irish Moss (grams)	3	3	3
Total liquor (litres)	26.9	32.6	35.4
Mash liquor (litres)	8.9	10.8	11.7

Mash schedule 66°C (151°F), 90 minutes

Boil time 90 minutes

Final gravity 1008

Alcohol content (ABV) 5.6%

Bitterness units (EBU) 40

Colour (EBC) 21

Malt extract version – Replace the pale malt with the appropriate quantity of pale-coloured, premium grade malt extract and brew using the malt extract brewing method.

	19 litres	23 litres	25 litres
Malt Extract Syrup (grams)	2480	3000	3620
or			
Dried Malt Extract (grams)	2130	2580	2810

YOUNG'S SPECIAL

Sweet citrus on the nose follows through into
a malty, hoppy flavour with a dry bitter
aftertaste and a touch of toffee.

ORIGINAL GRAVITY

1046

	19 litres	23 litres	25 litres
Pale Malt (grams)	3560	4310	4690
Crystal Malt (grams)	350	425	460
Start of Boil			
Fuggle Hops (grams)	22	27	29
Golding Hops (grams)	22	27	29
Last Ten Minutes of Boil			
Golding Hops (grams)	15	18	19
Irish Moss (grams)	3	3	3
Total liquor (litres)	27.2	33	35.8
Mash liquor (litres)	9.7	11.8	12.8

Mash schedule 66°C (151°F), 90 minutes

Boil time 90 minutes

Final gravity 1011

Alcohol content (ABV) 4.6%

Bitterness units (EBU) 32

Colour (EBC) 25

 Dry hop with a few cones of Target.

· ·

Malt extract version – Replace the pale malt with the appropriate quantity of pale-
coloured, premium grade malt extract and brew using the malt extract brewing method.

	19 litres	23 litres	25 litres
Malt Extract Syrup (grams)	2670	3230	3520
or			
Dried Malt Extract (grams)	2300	2780	3030

Porter & Stout Recipes

There is much myth and misconception surrounding Porter. This particularly enigmatic drink was the favourite of Londoners from the early 1700s until the mid to late nineteenth century when its popularity was superseded by pale ale.

It would be difficult, if not controversial, to try and define a traditional Porter. Its phenomenal success prompted virtually every brewer to jump on the bandwagon with his own imitation version. Add to this the fact that Porter's heyday lasted for well over 150 years and it becomes plain that the drink had more than enough time in which to evolve considerably. An eighteenth-century Porter would have been quite different to a nineteenth-century Porter. Any definition of Porter must also take into account regional variations. London Porter was regarded as the true Porter; the real stuff. Porter brewed in the countryside was nothing like London Porter; but it was still called Porter just the same. Modern Porters most closely resemble countryside Porters.

The original (early 1700s) London Porter was a mixture of Mild and stale beer. The terms 'mild' and 'stale' have changed popular meaning over the years. Mild meant fresh, young beer that had not been matured. It did not mean lightly-flavoured or mellow, nor lightly-hopped or weak, as in today's meaning. Indeed, Mild would have been harsh, possibly disagreeable stuff. Stale, on the other hand, meant exactly the opposite. It meant it had been stood, stored, matured and was old. The Mild was fresh stuff, virtually straight out of the brewery, and was cheap. The stale beer, on the other hand, was matured for a year or two until it developed a sub-acetic flavour that was much esteemed by Londoners, and was much more expensive.

This sub-acetic flavour was caused partly by bacteria, but the major part of the flavour of stale was produced by a secondary yeast that we know today as *Brettanomyces* (British Fungus). *Brettanomyces* activity did not occur during fermentation, but well into maturation when conditions became right for it, causing a secondary fermentation that required the pressure to be released in the maturation casks or butts. Today we would probably regard the stale as sour. It was observed, probably by the drinking public, that mixing a small proportion of stale beer with Mild produced a much more palatable drink at an affordable price. The publicans held Mild and stale and the drinker mixed these together in his tankard to give his preferred degree of tang.

Both the Mild and stale were made from 100% brown malt. Brown malt was the cheapest form of malt in those days, but was not particularly brown by today's standards. Unlike today's brown malt, old-time brown malt was a smoked malt which, for London Porter, was smoked over hornbeam.

So now we have the beginnings of a definition of a true London Porter. Firstly, the early London Porter would have had a smoky flavour and a peculiar bitterness contributed by the hornbeam-smoked brown malt from which it was made. Secondly it would have had a vinous, acetic quality imparted by the deliberate souring with a small portion of stale beer. Thirdly it was a translucent brown, not black.

During the 1700s Porter was progressively darkened to give the impression of strength, but by the early 1800s pale malt (an unsmoked malt) became cheaper than brown malt, due to the industrialisation of Britain providing plentiful supplies of anthracite and coke, which are relatively smokeless fuels. The percentage of brown malt in the grist was gradually reduced in favour of pale and amber malts, typically becoming 33 per cent each of pale, amber, and

brown. Black malt was introduced to provide the colour and a peculiar bitterness. The smokiness would have reduced progressively too, with the reduction of brown malt. The souring now took place at the brewery by mixing about ten per cent stale with the Mild. The amber malt was gradually reduced down to zero and replaced with pale. The grist generally became pale, brown and black malts.

Early 19th century Porter was described thus: 'The qualities of the Porter at present admired are, perfect brilliancy, a dark brown colour approaching to black, considerable bitterness, with a fine empyreumatic flavour, and a close creamy head. Without these requisites, Porter is little valued.' (*A Practical Treatise on Brewing*; Thomas Hitchcock, 1842). It is not clear whether empyreumatic refers to smoky or burnt. Both flavours would doubtless have been present.

By the mid to late 1900s there were several variations of Porter. The London brewers still used a proportion of brown malt; the last batch of proper old-time brown malt was made by French and Jupp in the 1950s and was used in Mackeson. The London brewers also still soured their Porter well into the twentieth century; bottled Guinness was still being soured in the 1980s, and it is rumoured that its Foreign Extra Stout still is. Many brewers only finally demolished their huge souring vats in the twentieth century.

Porter made in the provinces was rarely the same as London Porter and was really a Porter look-alike, rather than the real thing. It is difficult to be specific, because techniques varied, but it is certain that the souring was absent in many cases, and the drink was just a dark, bitter, beer. The grist, like today's Porter, would have been mostly pale malt with the addition of coloured malts

Today's Porters are not really Porters at all in the strict sense of the word. They are not smoky, nor are they soured, but consist mostly of pale malt with black and brown and chocolate malts to provide additional flavour. It should be pointed out that modern brown and amber malts are not the same as old-time brown and ambers, so recreating an authentic Porter would be difficult these days, but then I would be surprised if a real Porter, made as it was 150 years ago, would find favour with many modern palates.

Probably the biggest unsolved mystery is how Porter got its name, and we will still be speculating about it for years to come. The usual explanation is that it was named for the London street porters, and that is as good an explanation as any, but I don't really believe it.

My own guess that Porter is a corruption of the Latin *potare*, which was probably chalked on the casks when the beer had matured enough and was fit to drink – *potare* in the sense of potable. While we are on the subject of Latin there is the (unlikely) possibility that it is a corruption of *portio*, meaning portion, or part.

Porter, after all, was originally one part stale to two parts Mild.

The most likely origin of the name is in port. Port is a fortified wine. Porter is a Mild beer fortified with a small portion of strong stale beer. Due to England's frequent punch-ups with France and Germany, Portuguese wine was the major wine in Britain from about the late seventeenth century onwards. These wines did not travel well, so the traders added brandy to 'fortify' them against the rigours of their Atlantic sea voyage. The pioneers of the Port trade soon found the fortifying process did far more than just protect the wine. It improved it, giving it the power to mature into something unique. Just like Porter.

Stout began life as a stronger version of any beer, but eventually became exclusively to mean a stronger version of Porter. Stout has changed over the years, and has, with a couple of exceptions, moved quite a long way from its origins. The notion that Stout was full of goodness encouraged the practice of prescribing Stout for medicinal purposes, and this in turn brought about a trend in 'food Stouts' which became very popular because of their supposed nutritional benefit. Invalid Stout, tonic Stout, oatmeal Stout, oyster Stout, butter Stout, milk Stout and sweet Stout are the most common examples, but they have nearly all disappeared now. Mackeson, a milk Stout, is still available – just, and one or two micros produce an oatmeal Stout.

★
BATEMANS SALEM PORTER

Ruby black with a brown tint to the head. The aroma is liquorice with a subtle hint of dandelion and burdock; the initial taste is hoppy and bitter, with a mellowing of all the elements in the finish.

ORIGINAL GRAVITY
1048

	19 litres	23 litres	25 litres
Pale Malt (grams)	2750	3320	3610
White Sugar (grams)	455	550	600
Crystal Malt (grams)	420	505	550
Roasted Barley (grams)	190	230	250

Start of Boil

Challenger Hops (grams)	36	43	47

Last Ten Minutes of Boil

Golding Hops (grams)	12	14	15
Irish Moss (grams)	3	3	3

Total liquor (litres)	26.7	32.4	35.2
Mash liquor (litres)	8.4	10.2	11

Mash schedule 66°C (151°F), 90 minutes
Boil time 90 minutes
Final gravity 1009
Alcohol content (ABV) 5.2%
Bitterness units (EBU) 36
Colour (EBC) 129

• •

Malt extract version – Replace the pale malt with the appropriate quantity of pale-coloured, premium grade malt extract and brew using the malt extract brewing method.

	19 litres	23 litres	25 litres
Malt Extract Syrup (grams)	2060	2490	2710
or			
Dried Malt Extract (grams)	1770	2140	2330

BURTON BRIDGE TOP DOG STOUT

Black and rich with a roast and malty start. Very
fruity. Abundant hops give a fruity, bitter finish with a
mouth-watering edge.

ORIGINAL GRAVITY

1050

	19 litres	23 litres	25 litres
Pale Malt (grams)	3120	3770	4100
Torrefied Wheat (grams)	905	1100	1200
Chocolate Malt (grams)	300	365	395
Start of Boil			
Challenger Hops (grams)	17	20	22
Total liquor (litres)	27.6	33.5	36.4
Mash liquor (litres)	10.8	13.1	14.2

Mash schedule 66°C (151°F), 90 minutes

Boil time 90 minutes

Final gravity 1013

Alcohol content (ABV) 4.9%

Bitterness units (EBU) 40

Colour (EBC) 133

CALEDONIAN PORTER

A dark, delectable brew from the Caledonian brewery
in Edinburgh. Biscuity in the mouth, dry finish with good hop character.

ORIGINAL GRAVITY
1042

	19 litres	23 litres	25 litres
Pale Malt (grams)	2730	3310	3600
Wheat Malt (grams)	385	465	510
Amber Malt (grams)	175	210	230
Crystal Malt (grams)	175	210	230
Chocolate Malt (grams)	110	135	150
Start of Boil			
Fuggle Hops (grams)	24	29	32
Golding Hops (grams)	24	29	32
Last Ten Minutes of Boil			
Irish Moss (grams)	3	3	3
Total liquor (litres)	26.9	32.6	35.4
Mash liquor (litres)	9	10.9	11.8

Mash schedule 66°C (151°F), 90 minutes
Boil time 90 minutes
Final gravity 1011
Alcohol content (ABV) 4.1%
Bitterness units (EBU) 35
Colour (EBC) 66

PORTER & STOUT RECIPES

★
FULLER'S LONDON PORTER

Rich and flavoursome dark ale based on an 1880s Fuller's recipe. Fuggles hop aroma with hints of coffee and chocolate. Dark malt and coffee in the mouth; long complex finish with earthy Fuggles and liquorice maltiness.

ORIGINAL GRAVITY
1053

	19 litres	23 litres	25 litres
Pale Malt (grams)	3490	4230	4590
Brown Malt (grams)	550	665	725
Crystal Malt (grams)	455	555	600
Chocolate Malt (grams)	92	110	120

Start of Boil

Fuggle Hops (grams)	53	64	70

Last Ten Minutes of Boil

Fuggle Hops (grams)	18	21	23

Total liquor (litres)	28	33.9	36.8
Mash liquor (litres)	11.4	13.9	15.1

Mash schedule 66°C (151°F), 90 minutes
Boil time 90 minutes
Final gravity 1014
Alcohol content (ABV) 5.2%
Bitterness units (EBU) 33
Colour (EBC) 100

GUINNESS EXTRA STOUT

A world classic beer of enormous complexity and character.

ORIGINAL GRAVITY
1042

	19 litres	23 litres	25 litres
Pale Malt (grams)	2590	3140	3410
Flaked Barley (grams)	740	895	975
Roasted Barley (grams)	370	445	485

Start of Boil

	19 litres	23 litres	25 litres
Target Hops (grams)	29	35	38
Total liquor (litres)	27	32.8	35.6
Mash liquor (litres)	9.2	11.2	12.1

Mash schedule 66°C (151°F), 90 minutes
Boil time 90 minutes
Final gravity 1013
Alcohol content (ABV) 3.8%
Bitterness units (EBU) 45
Colour (EBC) 203

★
RINGWOOD XXXX PORTER

Smooth, dark beer with superb roast malt character and a
rich hop and roast malt aroma. Dry in the mouth with burnt
malt notes and a hint of liquorice; dry nutty finish.

ORIGINAL GRAVITY
1048

	19 litres	23 litres	25 litres
Pale Malt (grams)	3300	4000	4350
Crystal Malt (grams)	330	400	435
Torrefied Wheat (grams)	330	400	435
Chocolate Malt (grams)	165	200	215
Start of Boil			
Challenger Hops (grams)	30	36	39
Last Ten Minutes of Boil			
Progress Hops (grams)	10	12	13
Post-boil Hops			
Golding Hops (grams)	6	7	8
Total liquor (litres)	27.5	33.3	36.1
Mash liquor (litres)	10.3	12.5	13.5

Mash schedule 66°C (151°F), 90 minutes

Boil time 90 minutes

Final gravity 1013

Alcohol content (ABV) 4.6%

Bitterness units (EBU) 30

Colour (EBC) 93

Appendices

Hydrometer temperature correction

When a hydrometer is used to measure fluids at a temperature other than its calibration temperature, a correction factor needs to be applied. The tables below give appropriate correction factors. Numbers preceded by a minus sign are subtracted from the hydrometer reading; the other numbers are added. For example: if a 20° hydrometer is used to measure wort which is at 26°C, then 0.0014 is added to the specific gravity reading (or 1.4 brewers' degrees, depending upon your point of view).

TEMPERATURE CORRECTION TABLE FOR 15.6°C (60°F) HYDROMETERS				TEMPERATURE CORRECTION TABLE FOR 20°C HYDROMETERS			
0°C	-0.0008	25°C	0.002	0°C	-0.0016	25°C	0.0012
1°C	-0.0009	26°C	0.0022	1°C	-0.0017	26°C	0.0014
2°C	-0.0009	27°C	0.0025	2°C	-0.0017	27°C	0.0017
3°C	-0.001	28°C	0.0028	3°C	-0.0018	28°C	0.002
4°C	-0.0009	29°C	0.0031	4°C	-0.0018	29°C	0.0023
5°C	-0.0009	30°C	0.0034	5°C	-0.0018	30°C	0.0026
6°C	-0.0009	31°C	0.0037	6°C	-0.0017	31°C	0.0029
7°C	-0.0009	32°C	0.004	7°C	-0.0017	32°C	0.0032
8°C	-0.0008	33°C	0.0043	8°C	-0.0016	33°C	0.0035
9°C	-0.0008	34°C	0.0047	9°C	-0.0016	34°C	0.0039
10°C	-0.0007	35°C	0.005	10°C	-0.0015	35°C	0.0042
11°C	-0.0006	36°C	0.0054	11°C	-0.0014	36°C	0.0045
12°C	-0.0005	37°C	0.0057	12°C	-0.0013	37°C	0.0049
13°C	-0.0004	38°C	0.0061	13°C	-0.0012	38°C	0.0053
14°C	-0.0002	39°C	0.0065	14°C	-0.001	39°C	0.0056
15°C	-0.0001	40°C	0.0068	15°C	-0.0009	40°C	0.006
16°C	0.0001	41°C	0.0072	16°C	-0.0007	41°C	0.0064
17°C	0.0002	42°C	0.0076	17°C	-0.0006	42°C	0.0068
18°C	0.0004	43°C	0.008	18°C	-0.0004	43°C	0.0072
19°C	0.0006	44°C	0.0085	19°C	-0.0002	44°C	0.0076
20°C	0.0008	45°C	0.0089	20°C	0	45°C	0.0081
21°C	0.001	46°C	0.0093	21°C	0.0002	46°C	0.0085
22°C	0.0012	47°C	0.0098	22°C	0.0004	47°C	0.0089
23°C	0.0015	48°C	0.0102	23°C	0.0007	48°C	0.0094
24°C	0.0017	49°C	0.0107	24°C	0.0009	49°C	0.0098

Conversions

One level teaspoon (5 ml) holds the following approximate weights of the specified substances:

Calcium Carbonate	1.8 grams
Calcium Chloride	3.4 grams
Gypsum	4 grams
Epsom Salts	4.5 grams
Sodium Bicarbonate	4.5 grams
Irish moss (fine)	3 grams

A domestic teaspoon holds approximately: 5 ml
A domestic dessert spoon holds approximately: 10 ml
A domestic tablespoon holds approximately: 15 ml
A large coffee mug holds approximately: 300 ml

19 litres = 4.2 Imp. gallons = 5 US gallons = 33.4 pints
23 litres = 5.1 Imp. gallons = 6.1 US gallons = 40.5 pints
25 litres = 5.5 Imp. gallons = 6.6 US gallons = 44 pints

To convert:

Grams to ounces	Multiply by 0.035
Kilograms to pounds	Multiply by 2.205
Litres to fluid ounces (UK)	Multiply by 35.195
Litres to cups (US)	Multiply by 4.227
Litres to pints (UK)	Multiply by 1.76
Litres to quarts (US)	Multiply by 1.057
Litres to gallons (US)	Multiply by 0.264
Litres to gallons (Imp.)	Multiply by 0.22
Litres to barrels (UK)	Multiply by 0.006
Litres to hogsheads (UK)	Multiply by 0.003

To convert the other way, divide by the figure shown

°C to °F Multiply by 1.8 then add 32

1 part per million (ppm) = 1 miligram per litre (mg/l)
= 1 millilitre per litre (ml/l)

Internet resources

A good place to improve your knowledge and see what others get up to is a home-brewing forum. The better, well-mannered ones usually have a good sprinkling of people who are willing to dish out help and advice. A good and well-attended British home brewing forum is: www. jimsbeerkit.co.uk.

The major British home brewers' organisation is the Craft Brewing Association. It is an unfortunate name because it gives the impression that it is a commercial micro-brewer's organisation, whereas it is primarily a home brewer's group. The Craft Brewing Association has a number of regional sub-groups through which members meet up It also issues a quarterly printed magazine. The CBA can be found at: www.craftbrewing. org.uk.

You may wish to look at my web site at: www.practicalbrewing.co.uk, if only to see if there is anything ground-breaking on it yet. You can certainly download my freebee "BeerEngine" brewing software which will enable you to modify the recipes within this book or even help you to design your own. There is also a water-treatment calculator for the more experienced home brewer.

Beer Index

Index

Books for Beer Lovers

Good Beer Guide 2012

Editor: Roger Protz

The *Good Beer Guide* is the only guide you will ever need to find the right pint, in the right place, every time. It's the original and best-selling guide to around 4,500 pubs throughout the UK. Now in its 39th year, this annual publication is a comprehensive and informative guide to the best real ale pubs in the UK, researched and written exclusively by CAMRA members and fully updated every year.

£15.99   **ISBN 978-1-85249-266-3**

Good Bottled Beer Guide

Jeff Evans

A pocket-sized guide for discerning drinkers looking to buy bottled real ales and enjoy a fresh glass of their favourite beers at home. The 7th edition of the Good Bottled Beer Guide is completely revised, updated and redesigned to showcase the very best bottled British real ales now being produced, and detail where they can be bought. Everything you need to know about bottled beers; tasting notes, ingredients, brewery details, and a glossary to help the reader understand more about them.

£12.99   **ISBN 978-1-85249-262-5**

Book of Beer Knowledge

Jeff Evans

An absorbing, pocket-sized book, packed with beer facts, feats, records, stats and anecdotes – you'll never be lost for words at the pub again. Covering everything from the serious (how do you spot faults in beer?) to the silly (where can you buy beer for dogs?), this book will both inform and entertain.

£7.99   **ISBN 978-1-85249-292-2**

Great British Pubs

Adrian Tierney-Jones

Great British Pubs is a celebration of the British pub. This fully illustrated and practical book presents the pub as an ultimate destination – featuring pubs everyone should seek out and make a visit to. It recommends a selection of the very best pubs in various different categories, as chosen by leading beer writer Adrian Tierney-Jones.

£14.99   **ISBN 978-1-85249-265-6**

Order these and other CAMRA books online at **www.camra.org.uk/books**, ask at your local bookstore, or contact: CAMRA, 230 Hatfield Road, St Albans, AL1 4LW. Telephone 01727 867201

A Campaign of Two Halves

Campaigning for Pub Goers & Beer Drinkers

CAMRA, the Campaign for Real Ale, is an independent not-for-profit, volunteer-led consumer group. We campaign tirelessly for good-quality real ale and pubs, as well as lobbying government to champion drinkers' rights and promote local pubs as centres of community life. As a CAMRA member you will have the opportunity to campaign to save pubs under threat of closure, for pubs to be free to serve a range of real ales at fair prices and for a reduction in beer duty that will help Britain's brewing industry survive.

Enjoying Real Ale & Pubs

CAMRA has over 130,000 members from all ages and backgrounds, brought together by a common belief in the issues that CAMRA deals with and their love of good quality British beer. From just £20 a year – that's less than a pint a month – you can join CAMRA and enjoy the following benefits:

Subscription to *What's Brewing*, our monthly colour newspaper, and *Beer*, our quarterly magazine, informing you about beer and pub news and detailing events and beer festivals around the country.

Free or reduced entry to over 160 national, regional and local beer festivals.

Money off many of our publications including the *Good Beer Guide*, the *Good Bottled Beer Guide* and *CAMRA's Great British Pubs*.

Access to a members-only section of our national website, **www.camra.org.uk**, which gives up-to-the-minute news stories and includes a special offer section with regular features.

Special discounts with numerous partner organisations and money off real ale in your participating local pubs as part of our Pubs Discount Scheme.

Log onto **www.camra.org.uk/joinus** for
CAMRA membership information.

CAMPAIGN
FOR
REAL ALE